Restoring Civility: Lessons from the Master

Nels — God bless you and your whole family! I thank God for you, your friendship, support, prayers and spiritual depth.

Kent

**Attention:
Civility can be
good for your
health**

Also by Kent R. Hunter

Who Broke My Church? 7 Proven Strategies for Renewal and Revival

Discover Your Windows: Lining Up with God's Vision

Your Spiritual Gifts: Discover God's Plan for Your Life

The J-Dog Journey: Where Is Life?

The Jesus Enterprise: Engaging Culture to Reach the Unchurched

Your Church Has Personality: Find Your Focus – Maximize Your Mission

Restoring Civility: Lessons from the Master

Your Path to Rediscover Respect

Kent R. Hunter

with Tracee J. Swank

Church Doctor Ministries

Corunna, Indiana

Dedicated to my wife, Janet

"Remind the people to respect the government and be law-abiding, always ready to lend a helping hand. No insults, no fights, God's people should be bighearted and courteous."

Titus 3:1-2
The Message

CONTENTS

INTRODUCTION
Pain-Free Progress

"The day may dawn when fair play, love for one's fellow men, respect for justice and freedom will enable tormented generations to march forth triumphant from the hideous epoch in which we have to dwell. Meanwhile, never flinch, never weary, never despair."

— Winston Churchill[1]

His last speech to the British House of Commons, March 1, 1955

When Winston Churchill made this comment, he reflected on the deterioration of civilized respect. It was 1955. It would be impossible for Churchill—or anyone in the 1955 world—to fathom our technological world today.

It was over dinner that Ray Day shared his view about the challenges humans face. At the time, Ray was vice president of communications for Ford Motor Company. (He is now the chief communications officer for IBM.) We had worked with the congregation he attended. Ray served as the "internal coordinator." He got his church ready for our onsite visit. He oversaw the distribution of our analytical surveys.

My colleague, Tracee, and I shared with Ray our observation: Violations of polite communication have skyrocketed. We reflected on the drift of behavior in the media among celebrities, politicians, and students in the classroom. We were shocked it could occur also in churches. Wouldn't Christians know better?

Ray shared a concept that clarifies. He called it "citizen journalism." He explained, "The electronic revolution allows anyone to multiply communication. This makes everyone an amateur journalist." Journalists are trained to represent certain ethical standards. They also operate under the scrutiny of their readers. If they get sloppy, they lose readers, sales go down, and they get fired. There is a mechanism of discipline.

However, in this world of citizen journalists, there are few checks and balances. There is liberty without discipline. You can say whatever you want to an unlimited number of people. Now, many professional journalists have adjusted to this "liberty." Technology makes communication easier. Yet, it requires an internal compass—more than ever. Without discipline, respect disintegrates. Society implodes! *"Free speech" requires mature responsibility.*

This book provides you with a map to relocate your compass. There are lessons from the genius, Jesus, to help you become a better you. It is your opportunity to be a champion for civility.

The dictionary defines *civility* as politeness in acts and speech. If you are civilized, you belong to "a social organization of a high order: advanced in language, arts, sciences, and government." To *civilize* means "to come out of a primitive or savage condition." Civility is all about respect.

How do you know you can look back at the end of your life, focus on those you touched, and say, "Well done; they are better

INTRODUCTION

because I lived"? How do you interact with others? It depends on your compass. What are your boundaries before you speak, text, or email?

How do you get along with others? If you're bumper to bumper in the fast lane of life, it's time to pull over and self-reflect. Take a pause. Look back to the future. It could be the most valuable moment of your life.

As you read, focus with me on the undisputed most influential person in history. His name was Jesus. On the historical record, He could be considered the greatest influence on the subject of civility in history. Do you know why?

Jesus started the largest, longest-lasting, most impactful movement ever. No other movement, ideology, or approach comes close. It doesn't matter what you measure: longevity of His movement, number of followers, or the impact on civilization. His followers have initiated hospitals, orphanages, schools, civil rights, economic methods, structure of governments, and humanitarian efforts. That is a lot of influence!

There are some who self-identify as "Christians" who don't reflect Jesus' teachings. Don't get hung up on that. There's a difference between being forgiven and being perfect. There are abusers of civil communication, even in churches. Their behavior may be out of ignorance of what Jesus taught. They need to learn more about Jesus. Or, they may be overwhelmed by technology. What about you?

Jesus said, "Because of the increase of wickedness, the love of most grows cold."[2] Look at this: *What did Jesus teach about how we should get along?* What did He teach about how human beings should treat one another? What are the behavioral nuggets that enhance communication, comradery, problem solving? *How can we disagree without being disagreeable?* The answer is spiritual and strategic. Look at Jesus' approach to people—beggars, even enemies. His approach is transformative, powerful, effective, and transferable.

You can do this! You can add value to others through better behavior. You can grow into respectful interaction. If you do, everyone wins! Respect is powerful. Respect given is respect earned. *Respect is a movement.* It begins with you...and me.

The impact of Jesus on this world is unparalleled. He focused on *culture*. He called this culture the "Kingdom of God." He infused culture into His followers. They *caught* it even more than He taught it. He modeled it. It was beyond academic. It was infectious.

Good behavior—the transformational kind—rubs off on people. If you diagnose Jesus' teachings and actions, they contain five important elements: (1) values; (2) beliefs; (3) attitudes; (4) priorities; and (5) worldviews. I've written about this in my book *Who Broke My Church? 7 Proven Strategies for Renewal and Revival.*[3] These seeds of greatness are for you. Jesus' culture improves everyone.

Jesus used stories to describe how this culture works. He understood the power of story. If you want to build a positive culture, you will become a great storyteller. Want an example? What do influencing parents do with their little children? They read them stories! What do effective politicians do in speeches? They use uplifting narratives. Think of recent U.S. presidents as they spoke about the state of the union.

They often point out an individual in the gallery and tell their story. Their speechwriters get it: The impact of story is the power of influence. Think about great leaders throughout history: Every one is a great storyteller. Jesus was one of the best.

Stories represent the vehicle. They reflect your values, beliefs, attitudes, priorities, and worldviews. They reflect your compass. They *fuel* culture-based decisions. They *clarify* discussions and debates. Cultural components reduce noise. They clear the fog. They set the stage for respectful relationships—a civil society.

Respect is the foundation of civilization. It separates those who are civilized from those who are not. It is the issue of behavior. Respect separates human beings from animals.

Civility reflects decency, kindness, and generous care for others. It produces selfless love, purpose, honor, forgiveness, and restoration. Civility is the platform of politeness. It is more about the common good than about the success of personal opinion. Is that you?

President John F. Kennedy said, "Ask not what your country can do for you. Ask what you can do for your country."[4] This goes beyond party spirit, selfishness, or personal opinion. This vision for the common good challenges you to rise above a self-centered perspective like, "The world revolves around me."

In the November 2018 issue of the *Journal of Personality and Social Psychology*, research cited that Congress is evaluated more positively by citizens when civil discourse is evident.[5] Respect is embedded in the uniqueness of human beings.

When civility wanes in society, a frequent reaction is, "We need more rules." It is a foolish attempt to legislate morality. It is a shallow approach to replace civility. It creates bureaucracy which diminishes productivity. Do you look for government to impose civility?

Eventually, it leads to socialism, the theory that a system can replace personal, relational civility. It cannot.

On May 20, 2017, Vice President Mike Pence delivered the commencement address for graduates of Pennsylvania's Grove City College. Pence told the graduates, "Servant leadership, not selfish ambition, must be the animating force of the career that lies before you."[6] What is the source of Mike Pence's worldview? The article says, "...his evangelical beliefs." More accurately, the source is Jesus Christ, the Master of civility.

In Matthew 7:24-25, Jesus taught about building a house on a stone foundation. It will survive the storms. In contrast, building a house on sand will destruct. The "house" can be applied personally. Reflect on yourself. The "house" also fits society. Whether the society acts in a civil or an uncivil way, it reflects the foundation. A person without civility will collapse in the face of storms. The same is true of a society.

In November of 1620, the Mayflower Compact was signed by those on an English ship prior to landing at Plymouth, Massachusetts. It was the first framework of government enacted in the territory now called the United States of America. It was a pledge "for the greater good."

The Mayflower Compact was not a constitution, but rather an adaptation of a Puritan church covenant to a civil situation. Civility, grounded in spiritual authority, was the foundation for what would become the United States of America. The Compact says:

Having undertaken, for the Glory of God, and the advancement of the Christian faith...do by these present solemnly and mutually in the presence of God and one another, covenant, and combine ourselves together into a *civil body politic*...for the general good of the colony: unto which we promise all due submission and obedience....[7]

The Christian faith provides a cultural compass. It directed those who came to North America to form "a more perfect union." Jesus clearly understood that human beings aren't perfect. However, through faith in Him, they receive forgiveness. They can practice these basic elements of civility: love, respect, humility, honor, selflessness, servanthood, grace, kindness, goodness, and acceptance. Would you like to see more of those qualities?

The source of civility is spiritual.

The result of civility is character.

The nature of civility is servanthood.

The purpose of civility is preservation.

The motive of civility is love.

The measure of civility is sacrifice.

The power of civility is forgiveness.

The authority of civility is submission.

The privilege of civility is honor.

The strength of civility is humility.

The foundation of civility is Jesus Christ.

INTRODUCTION

Where you sow civility, you harvest harmony. Where you invest in harmony, you experience community. Where you build community, you enjoy progress. Progress is a sacred trust given by your Creator. In the Bible, the apostle Paul writes:

> But what happens when we live God's way? He brings gifts into our lives, much the same way that fruit appears in an orchard—things like affection for others, exuberance about life, serenity. We develop a willingness to stick with things, a sense of compassion in the heart, and a conviction that a basic holiness permeates things and people. We find ourselves involved in loyal commitments, not needing to force our way in life, able to marshal and direct our energies wisely. Legalism is helpless in bringing this about; it only gets in the way.[8]

In Chapter One, the focus is on behavior. This dynamic of life divides or unifies. In Chapter Two, we look at the powerful influence of Jesus, who transforms behavior. Chapter Three reveals the first of seven civility lessons taught by Jesus: You influence others. Chapter Four focuses on the second lesson: the dynamic power of significance, which is a prerequisite for success. Chapter Five unpacks the third lesson that refreshes genuine respect, humility. Chapter Six is about organic living, the element of growth that produces results, the centerpiece of Jesus' lesson number four. Chapter Seven provides Jesus' fifth lesson: ways to build respect. Chapter Eight recognizes Jesus, the master storyteller, and the importance of your story. This is all about the power of story. Chapter Nine is about the art of respectful discourse, which is the seventh lesson we learn from Jesus. Chapter Ten provides the road map and challenge, as well as the benefits of a refreshed culture of respect.

Chapter One

Behavior 101

"Treat everyone you meet with dignity. Revere God. Respect the government."

— The Apostle Peter[1]

The alarm went off at 6:10 a.m. I jumped to turn it off, in a leap from sleep to reality. "Oh, yeah, I need to get to the airport," I remembered. I glanced out the bathroom window. "No snow. Great. No problem with traffic." I powered up my phone—the symbol of invasive life. How many texts? Any urgent emails?

OK, turn on the national news. I watch while I shave—isn't it normal, to multitask? So much to do, so little time. What's that about Washington, D.C.? "A swamp?" Leaders bickering. A lot of tension. Are leaders...leading?

Oh, politicians. Gridlock. I hit the shower. "Hey," I thought, "What is it with our leaders? Why is it so difficult to get anything done? What's the issue? What's the issue behind the issue? What's the solution? More laws?" What was it David Burkus wrote? It was: "People typically do not look to written codes for clues about how to behave; they look to others."[2]

Behavior Check

Where are you on the respect meter? Do you respect the speed limit—or cheat upward a few miles per hour? Is it about the rule of law or the protection of others—and yourself? Is it about respect for life—yours and others? What is the *real* reason we have laws? Are they to slow us down or help us respect others? Or, is it about respect for life?

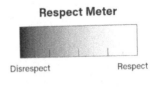

Respect Meter

Disrespect   Respect

Every group of people develops a culture. Every person, at every level, impacts the group. Whether you are a family or a country, you have a culture. Everyone and every action—even every thought—strengthens or weakens the whole group. I drove past Spring Arbor University in Spring Arbor, Michigan, and saw this on their sign: "Your life either sheds light or casts a shadow."[3] What about your life? Light or shadow? Likely, some of both, if you're honest.

When people group together, the immediate challenge is to get along. This is true of a married couple. In the first days of our married life, my wife clarified, "Your dirty clothes go in the hamper, not on the floor." I wanted to get along. I changed. But there is more. Civility is defined as "politeness, courtesy, especially in a formal way." The concept is related to "civilization." It's an approach that is civilized. Being uncivilized is to settle for less—below your culture. Instead of learning, improving, and moving forward, civilization stalls. How is it that otherwise intelligent human beings get to the level of gridlock? How does civilization deteriorate?

It's an issue of cultural drift. You could call it "Behavior 101." It can occur in every group—even whole nations. In history, there have been many empires: Rome, Egypt, Greece—and many more. Where are they today? They are shadows of their former "days of glory." It's the historical pattern of cultural drift. What made them strong was corrupted. They crumbled from self-destruction. It's a complex issue in every case. Do you think the decline of civility plays a role?

Civility is contagious. So is drift from civility. Respect in relationships is caught. So is disrespect. You impact others more than you know. I have never met the person who plows the snow on our road, but he or she impacts my day, one way or another. If the road is plowed, I get to the airport. If not, I can't. If I can't, that impacts someone who doesn't even live on my road! I'm thankful for those who plow and who respect their work—enough to get up in the middle of the night. They show respect to all those who live on our road. Civility multiplies. It travels like good news. Civility travels like laughter. Incivility travels like the flu.

Civilized culture is caught, not just taught. It is a cultural movement. Perhaps that's one of the reasons many countries have come…and gone, but a movement, like Christianity, continues. Whatever shapes good behavior develops productive and sustainable community. Yet, even some churches die. Our research shows the real issue is cultural drift.

This is huge. It seems so easy to lose the handle on civility. Cultural values have deep implications. They represent high responsibilities. Look at television commercials. Think about that new

> **Cultural values have deep implications.**

car a man sees advertised. The message implies, subliminally, if you buy the classy car, it comes with a sexy woman. Your testosterone just got manipulated!

Respect—or loss of respect—can be subtle. The dad says to his eight-year-old son, "Time for bed. Go put your pajamas on, and I'll come and tuck you in." The kid says, "Can I have a cookie?" Dad replies, "If I give you a cookie, will you get ready for bed?" The question? Who is influencing whom? If the pattern continues, will the son one day try to manipulate the legal system? His boss? If he does, there will be a crack in the civil culture of the company—and the son. Every action, every reaction, has consequences, ever so small, on civilized society.

To walk through life with a compass is to travel the high road of culture. It reflects respect. Your life is based on values, not bribes—or manipulation. Civilized behavior is powerful. Ralph Waldo Emerson asked a powerful question: "Who shall set a limit to the influence of a human being?"[4] Who do you influence?

Civil Reboot and Jesus' Approach

What do you think? Is it possible we need a civility "revival"? Would that impact our politicians? Corporations? Churches? Law enforcement? Hollywood? Schools? Universities? Nation? How would it mold and shape the next generation of children? Civility is a complex issue. In the Bible, respect is a divine attribute. The Scripture says, "If I speak with human eloquence and angelic ecstasy but don't love, I'm nothing but the creaking of a rusty gate."[5]

Those who submit to the culture of their society are called "civilians." The implication is that they are civilized to the standards that make that society great. Good civilians are on a mission. Whatever they do, there is direction. They operate with the cultural compass. It guides their values. It shapes their beliefs. It drives their behavior. The compass impacts their attitudes and shapes their priorities. It forms the way they see their world and the way the world works. It refines their life mission.

Steve Ballmer, who was CEO of Microsoft, spoke of the company's success. Ballmer said, "You can't just reorganize the company to make something like this happen. Anyway, we've probably had too many reorganizations around here. So it's really a question of re-missioning people rather than reorganizing them. Does that make sense?"[6] If you are a civilized person, you are not limited to *reactions*. You are on a mission. What is yours?

It seems counterintuitive, but Jesus' plan to influence His disciples began with the words, "Come, follow Me." Today, we might say, "Come, hang out with me for a while." People catch culture from others. Jesus gathered twelve ordinary men. He called them "disciples." They caught Jesus' high value of civility. Jesus' teachings and actions reflected a level of respect most had never encountered.

Jesus not only spoke to ten lepers. He touched them. He didn't just touch them, he healed them. Only one of the ten returned to thank Him. Ten lepers were healed. One was healed *and* caught the culture. This event changed all ten lepers, one more than the rest. It also changed the disciples who watched. They were moved to a whole new level of civility. They multiplied the movement that changed the Mediterranean world in the first century.

Jesus created a "spiritual epidemic." Many caught it. It eventually influenced and radically changed the Roman Empire. This movement has touched many nations. The words on the wall of the U.S. Congress still read, "In God we trust." Not everyone who serves there has grasped what that means, as it relates to their compass.

You can teach what you know, but you reproduce who you are. Jesus poured His life into twelve followers. He called it discipling, and they caught it. They became

> **You teach what you know, but you reproduce who you are.**

disciplers. Others caught the movement from them. The movement became contagious! Civilized behavior spreads the same way. So does uncivilized behavior!

Jim Collins, the author of the classic *Good to Great*, said, "A 30-second comment from a mentor can change your life forever."[7] This is why modeling civility is so effective: Respect is contagious. So, does it bother you that so many "leaders" treat one another in ways that publically reflect civil disobedience? If you're not sure, watch any newscast, or read a major newspaper or magazine. Civil leaders disagree without being disagreeable. Getting elected doesn't make you a civilized leader.

Do you know someone who is always focused on the quick fix? It doesn't work. Developing civility is a contagious, relational process. I remember what my mother said. She was in her 80s when she reminded me, "As long as you have children, you are a parent." She was saying that you impact your children until you die. She was an influence, not only to us, but to our children and also to their children. That's civil influence to three generations!

When George H.W. Bush, the 41st president of the United States, was laid to rest, we had the opportunity to learn two lessons: (1) He lived civility at a high level, a reflection of his faith in God. (2) His life of respect gained the respect of people everywhere. What will they say when they bury you?

A Movement of Love

Jesus spent His last three years building the most impactful movement in history. It seems unrealistic. Who would do that for three years with twelve ordinary guys? Who would expect the result? It became a movement impacting people on every continent—and still growing, 21 centuries later!

Have you ever heard this short but powerful verse in the Bible? "God is love."[8] We tend to put too much emphasis on the academic side of behavior. Jesus molded followers in an intimate relationship: "a band of brothers." They caught the culture that represents the highest form of civility—respectful behavior. That culture is called the Kingdom of God. They saw Jesus reach out to people in amazing ways. He said to the woman caught in the act of adultery, "You're forgiven." He gave sight to the blind, healed the sick, fed the hungry. He didn't fight the pagan Roman rulers that took over their land. He respected their leadership. His greatest challenge was the religious leaders! They had corrupted the culture of God's Kingdom. This consistent commitment to civility is a lesson, even for those who don't follow Him. It is also a lesson for those who do!

How strange! Many followers of Jesus today have no clue how He engineered the movement they claim as their own. The quick-fix syndrome has reduced many church leaders to a limited focus: teaching and preaching. Many have missed the miracle: how influence is *multiplied*.

As church consultants, we've worked with thousands of pastors. Many don't influence others the way their leader demonstrated! It's not a simple academic process. It's *relational apprenticing*. Jesus called it

7

"discipling." No one can "disciple" or "apprentice" a crowd. It's a relational connection. If you want others to grow into civility, follow Jesus' approach.

Civility or Civil War?

In the early years of the United States, many of the founders arrived with an inherited culture of owning slaves. Excuse the pun, but for many leaders, the issue wasn't as simple as "black and white." Thomas Jefferson inherited a farm that came with slaves. He eventually demonstrated a more inclusive position. The country fought a bitter war. It is still called the *Civil* War. Civility won the war but not the battle.

Many years later, Martin Luther King Jr. came on the scene. As a Christian, he was connected to *real* civility—at a higher level. He knew he had to be the very embodiment of the civil rights movement if he expected to make a difference. On one occasion, he said, "People cannot become devoted to Christianity until they find Christ, to democracy until they find Lincoln, Jefferson, and Roosevelt, to communism until they find Marx and Lenin and Stalin…. People are often led to causes, and often become committed to great ideas, through persons who personify those ideas."[9]

Consider the respect level of those who are elected officials. Or those who are popular in the music, film, or television industries. How civil do they act toward others who share a different worldview? How do they respect the laws? How do they respect other leaders?

One of Jesus' followers, Peter, became a great leader in the early years of the Christian movement. He wrote a couple of letters to church people. These letters are in the Bible. Remember, the recipients of Peter's letters were Christians who were forced to live under the rule of a pagan Roman emperor. The local leaders, from foreign Rome, were usually not Christians. These leaders had conquered the land. They collected taxes from people who were already poor. They sent most of the money to Rome. Yet, Peter writes, "Respect the authorities, whatever their level; they are God's emissaries for keeping order."[10] That is uncommon respect! Consider the challenges to Abraham Lincoln. What about the disrespect toward almost every president since? You can be civil and still disagree. However, disagreement is not a license to be disrespectful. Disrespect is not civil—it is uncivilized! What if politicians would disagree without being disagreeable?

Consider these words of Peter and his quote from Psalm 34:

> Be agreeable, be sympathetic, be loving, be compassionate, be humble.... No retaliation. No sharp-tongued sarcasm. Instead, bless—that's your job, to bless.... Whoever wants to embrace life and see the day fill up with good, here's what you do: Say nothing evil or hurtful; snub evil and cultivate good; run after peace for all your worth. God looks on all this with approval, listening and responding well to what he's asked; but he turns his back on those who do evil things.[11]

Moving the Compass Needle

Your impact on others can be for good or for harm. Some people in history are known for their positive impact. William Wilberforce worked tirelessly to abolish slavery in England. Abraham Lincoln took many risks, persisted, and finally ended slavery in America. Many missionaries, doctors, and nurses have faced significant dangers to bring physical relief and spiritual hope into hostile areas of the world.

Adolf Hitler was powerful. He convinced millions of people to give their lives for a horrible cause. He was a leader with a poor idea. Consider Hitler's values, beliefs, attitudes, priorities, and worldviews. Can you see how culture has consequences—for good or bad?

Not all people are bold, public figures. Some are quiet but brilliant scientists, working on vaccines, saving millions of lives. Others, like Mother Teresa, work among the poorest of the poor, showing love and compassion without fanfare or notoriety. In the end, she earned the admiration of millions. That tiny woman will be a giant in the history books for centuries!

Civility shapes behavior for those who move movements. Movements impact millions. The greatest movements are those that

> The greatest movements are those that multiply others.

multiply others, who raise up more influencers who multiply as well. This was Jesus' approach. His multiplication process is influence to the tenth power. Influencing others who become influencers leads to geometric progression. Would you like to see a movement of respect overcome our world?

If you could fold this page you're reading fifty times and stack it up on the floor, do you know how tall it would be? It would reach from here to the sun. And if you folded it one more time? It would reach from here to the sun and back. That is the power of multiplication:

people impacting others.[12] Civility is contagious. How you behave around your ten-year-old granddaughter has implications for dozens of heirs you will not live to meet. Yes, you do have the power to shape the world of respect! You *will* move the compass needle. The question is this: which direction?

Some say, "I don't really influence anyone." Oh, yes, you do! For good or for harm. To have no influence, you must live in a vacuum. Your

> **Civility is contagious.**

impact of respect doesn't even end when you die. When you respect others, your impact survives beyond your lifespan. Influence, for good or bad, continues long after you are gone. What will be your legacy?

I saw a newscast about a few elderly servicemen who survived the attack on Pearl Harbor. They were recognized at the White House. They don't know me, but they influenced me. They reflected their civil commitment. Even though I wasn't born yet, their story had an impact on me. Respect is powerful! It generates a better future for this world. Disrespect generates a bleak future. Where is the needle on your compass of civility? How will you contribute, starting now?

Yohan might describe himself as a hermit. He is Dutch by descent, but spent most of his life in South Africa. He then moved to Atlanta, Georgia. When his wife died, he moved to Anchorage, Alaska, and then to the wilderness, 200 miles from Fairbanks.

Yohan lives in a log cabin, alone: no phone, no Internet connection. His cabin is 48 miles from the nearest road. Being entirely self-sufficient, Yohan hasn't seen another person for 11 years. Does Yohan have any civil responsibility?

Yes, he does. Does he respect himself? What about the

environment? His survival, even in a remote place, may depend on his civil obedience to himself. Otherwise, he would drift toward being uncivilized. Civil obedience is healthy, even when no one is looking. People who discover the *why* of life enter the realm of significance.[13] They operate with the compass of civility.

Character

Civility is an issue of character. Character is the reflection of your compass, evident even when no one is looking. If you are polite, if

> **Character is the reflection of your compass.**

you have respect, it is who you *are* that drives what you *do*. Civility is demonstrated when no one is looking. If Yohan has a compass of civility, it impacts the way he treats his dog. Behavior has impact. Even self-respect matters.

William Faulkner said, "Don't bother just to be better than your contemporaries or predecessors. Try to be better than yourself."[14] The moment you stop learning, you stop growing. Your effectiveness begins to wane, whether or not you realize it. It is a character issue. Do you think you are smarter than you are? If you think you are better than you are, you lack humility (the subject of Chapter Five).

Or, perhaps, you suffer from false humility. You don't think you can learn. You don't believe you can change. You *are* but believe you can't *become*. You're wrong! And, if you're wrong, you're right: You can't learn. You can't change. You can't become. *You* are your greatest obstacle to your own self-respect.

On the issue of how we treat one another, we need a transformation. John Maxwell says,

People who are unwilling to grow are unwilling to change. They cling to what they think is right. They are 'always' right and that's what makes them wrong. They are afraid to be wrong. They are afraid to say, 'This doesn't work anymore.' This is the key to personal growth. However, once you get personal growth, and are open to grow, that is, change, that becomes a part of you, you never go back.[15]

When I was seven years old, my mother gave birth to my sister, Kim. Kim was born with cerebral palsy. She almost died during her first ten days. Do you ever wonder why bad things happen to good people? Sometimes it's a much needed lesson in character growth. At age seven, I didn't know the concept of character, but I saw a huge change in my father. In retrospect, he discovered his compass. It wasn't the one he used when hunting. It was the one that redirected his life.

My dad was, in many ways, my hero. He taught me how to fish, canoe, swim, cut the grass—not all "fun" stuff! Dad worked hard. Every deer season he would take his big gun (in the eyes of a seven-year-old) and travel north in Michigan. Most years he would return with a deer tied to the front hood of his car. He knew so many things, from the perspective of a young son. He actually built our first house himself, and that wasn't even his line of work. In those days, he repaired cash registers.

Every Sunday, when my mom took me to church and Sunday school, my dad would stay home and work on something. Yet, he changed the day my sister, Kim, was brought home—with little hope of living to age five. I'll never forget it. I walked into my parents' bedroom with great expectations. I'd never seen a baby sister. Even at seven, I could feel the tension in the air. Something wasn't right. Then I noticed my dad. He was on his knees. He was crying. I caught what he was saying, while sobbing: "Our baby is very sick and close to death...Oh God...help our baby."

Well, I believe God did help. My sister lived. That wasn't the only miracle. My dad changed. I couldn't describe it at that age, but now I get it. My dad, my superhero, got a cultural compass. His compass needle got transformed. He was different after that. It wasn't all at once. It was the start of his journey. He began attending church with us.

That's when dad began to grow in civility. He showed more respect for God and for others. In fact, that's when he began to influence me the most. I didn't realize it at the time, but people who attend church actually demonstrate a hunger to become...more. It's a sign they want to learn, want to grow. They don't know it all. Maybe they learn they aren't God. Perhaps they realize they aren't in charge of everything.

Years later, I read a line by Leighton Ford, who worked with Billy Graham. My dad watched Billy Graham crusades on TV after he changed. Leighton Ford said, "God loves us the way we are, but he loves us too much to leave us that way."[16] Real character takes off in flight when your life has direction. The compass needle moves.

All parents are influencers. The next generation is greatly influenced by today's parents. Teachers are great influencers. Can you name one who influenced you? I had a Sunday school teacher who impacted me greatly. It is an example of how civility rubs off. Her name was Mrs. Janetski. That's all I remember.

What I don't remember? How old I was. I don't know the names of other kids in that class. I can't remember the room or where it was located. I can't remember any particular lesson she taught. I just know she was a positive influence. It wasn't what she taught. *It was who she was.* That is cultural influence. At that young age, I caught a little of Mrs. Janetski. In a special way, that part of her is with me today.

Who has touched your life? Whose lives do you touch? Do they catch your compass culture—your values, beliefs, attitudes, priorities, and worldviews? Is your needle true north?

Many CEOs shape civil behavior. So do many managers. So does the janitor who cleans the shop floor. Everyone influences someone. The compass of respect impacts great companies. Civility builds great firefighters, soldiers, cab drivers, plumbers—everyone. It develops great countries. The civility compass significantly impacts the next generation. Parents: your role is significant. You're not just raising kids. You are shaping the world! It's not simply academic. Culture is caught.

Many people underestimate their potential for civil influence. Why? They don't consider themselves influencers. Think about the influential power of a waitress. Have you ever had a waitress who forgets a portion of your meal? By the time you get it, it's cold. Does that influence your eating pleasure? Absolutely! Does that influence the bottom line for the owner of the restaurant? Eventually, yes!

When my wife and I eat breakfast at Maria's, we will wait for an opening in Brenda's section. Why? Because Brenda is a civil influencer. How? She is an excellent waitress. Yet, we have never seen her résumé. We just know: Brenda has respect for others. She loves people. She is infectious. You catch it from her. Does that make her the most *efficient* waitress when she takes time to ask about our kids? Not really! Is she the most *effective* waitress at Maria's? Absolutely! Life is about a lot more than food—or "getting the job done." Brenda serves so much more than breakfast. She builds civility. She makes breakfast a welcome experience—no matter what you order.

How you treat people is vitally important. Your engagement with those in your social network is like sowing seeds. Whether good or bad, they grow and impact lives. Jesus had a man come up to Him and ask, "Teacher, what good thing must I do to get eternal life?" Jesus basically told him to follow the ten commandments, including "love your neighbor as you love yourself." The man left in despair. Later, the disciples who witnessed this conversation asked, "Then who has any chance at all?" Jesus answered, "No chance at all, if you think you can pull it off yourself. Every chance in the world if you trust God to do it."[17] The point? We're not perfect, but with God's help, we can show love and respect others.

Do you look at others with respect? Do you see yourself as a civil person? I once heard that 95 percent of those who influence you are those in your reference group. Your friends and family—those in your social network. They are your primary

> **With God's help, we can show love and respect.**

elevators. They either pick you up or take you down. This explains why three generations of relatives live in the ghetto. It's the reason why kids from certain families drop out of high school, one generation after another. It also describes how the drug culture and hate crimes often move from one person to the next. Would your friends describe you

16

as

an elevator? Does it matter? It does, in a civilized society. Think about the challenges facing our society. Which cultural elements are good? Which ones are bad? What about you? How do you fit?

You will walk in and out of the lives of many people during your lifetime. If you have underdeveloped civil influence, you will have less positive effect on them. If you have ignored your spiritual growth, you may be remembered as someone who walked all over them. If you have joined the never-ending process of becoming a civil encourager, think of all the people you will influence during your lifetime. You will leave footprints on their hearts, like Mrs. Janetski did for me. Wouldn't that make for a more civilized world? Mother Teresa once said, "We can do no great things, only small things with great love."[18]

Civility is more caught than taught; not like you catch a ball, but like you catch the flu. It is caught when you are up close

> **Civility is more caught than taught.**

and personal with others. In the next chapter, we'll look at the most influential person in history. And I hope you catch the genius of cultural architecture.

Chapter Two

The Master of Civility

"You did not choose me; I chose you and appointed you to go and bear much fruit, the kind of fruit that endures. And so the Father will give you whatever you ask of him in my name. This, then, is what I command you: love one another."

— Jesus[1]

Do you think our world could use a little more love? Thomas Jefferson said, "Every generation needs a new revolution."[2] The Civil War was physical, marked by bloodshed and loss of life. Other revolutions change lives more subtly, like the electronic revolution, anchored in the Internet. The most *dangerous* and most *beneficial* revolutions are cultural. Jesus' revolution is about love. Would life be improved if everyone would speak "the truth in love,..."[3]?

The Fall of Rome was a cultural revolution. In the first, second, and third centuries Rome had the most feared and well-equipped army in the world. The soldiers were both respected and feared. When you visit Rome, as well as many destinations in the Mediterranean world, you are moved by the splendor of structures and reminded that great empires can be conquered, even by themselves. The cancer of loveless human behavior is destructive.

For example, free speech is not a license to be rude. The confirmation hearings for Supreme Court Justice Brett Kavanaugh embarrassed U.S. civilization. From a nonpolitical, unbiased perspective, the spectacle of uncivilized behavior was a disgrace before the world. What's really strange? The word "civil" means "polite." "Polite" is related to the word "politics." How far have we wandered?

There are two ways a great nation can be conquered: (1) an enemy builds a bigger bomb, a stronger army, and develops smarter strategists, or (2) a nation crumbles from moral decay and civil dry rot. Mighty Rome was never conquered. It conquered itself. The culture lost the compass that made it great.

Do you have an active compass? You can have one type of compass that points the way. Or, you can have another kind that just draws circles. One moves forward. The other self-implodes.

If you follow a compass that points the way, life flourishes at every level. Following the compass

> **Follow a compass that points the way.**

that points true north gives direction. The quality of life is not about riches. There are more precious resources than financial wealth. They include peace, harmony, hope, joy, security—golden nuggets that aren't as easy to measure, but make the greater difference.

Do you think your country has simply a political divide? Or, do you see a cultural divide—a difference in values, beliefs, attitudes, priorities, and worldviews? If a nation misplaces the civil compass, other forces direct the people. That other compass drives a wedge through the population. Some follow true north; others are in a destructive spiral. A culture war emerges between the two compasses. Disruption follows. Those trying to steer the ship are shackled by gridlock. Civility is off the rails. Civilization is in jeopardy.

This confusing mess calls for you to perform at your very best. How do you do it? It is not so easy because the compass clash produces a great deal of fog. The only way out is for you to move out of the noise of dissonance. It is the rut of symptom solving. Henry David Thoreau said, "There are a thousand hacking at the branches of evil to one who is striking at the root."[4]

Consider the issues around abortion. People disagree about sensitive concepts. Can you be respectful to others? Reaching clarity on difficult issues challenges respect. People on opposite sides of this emotional issue tend to talk more than listen. It's easy to go into fast mode. Civility is the key to dialog, which is the platform for understanding. You *can* disagree without being disagreeable. For many, these challenges reflect our love for other human beings, no matter what their opinions or conclusions.

According to the Bible, God had one primary motive for sending Jesus into our world:

> This is how much God loved the world: He gave his Son, his one and only Son. And this is why: so that no one need be destroyed; by believing in him, anyone can have a whole and lasting life. God didn't go to all the trouble of sending his Son merely to point an accusing finger, telling the world how bad it was. He came to help, to put the world right again.[5]

Jesus is the master of civility. He died so we can live—forever. That is respect...and love.

What do you think is needed in a country where the number of suicides per year continues to grow? What about government gridlock? What about the rising level of anger and friction between worldviews of "left" and "right"? What do you think about people who, for no personal reason, walk up to a police officer and kill out of anger?

Are you so naïve to think the solution is simply passing more laws? If that was the complete solution, the prisons would be empty. Laws are an important element of social order. Laws are transactional. However, transformation is the bigger issue.

Transforming Behavior

In history, no one has demonstrated transforming civil respect as clearly as Jesus. Whether you are a Jesus-follower or not, His approach represents our most valuable model. Jesus began the longest-lasting movement in history. The sheer size of His movement, by numbers of followers, is amazing. Every other movement in history pales by comparison.

Christianity is also the most *influential* movement in history— 21 centuries and counting. It is a transformative explosion of the Judeo faith movement, which dates back to antiquity. No movement has produced more missionaries, hospitals, schools, and orphanages. Many nations have formed their governance approach from Judeo-Christian principles. The Christian movement is unparalleled.

Sadly, this is true: Many of Jesus' followers throughout history have abused or misused the basic elements of Jesus' movement. Jesus Himself taught that, by nature, His followers make mistakes and, by their own efforts, can never get to perfection this side of eternity.

His basic platform is not perfection but forgiveness. It is reconciliation that makes His followers strong. Christians confess two opposite claims: (1) Jesus was (and is) perfect. (2) Christians are not.

Jesus promises forgiveness and new life. His approach to culture provides a compass that has, and can, rescue nations, one person at a time. George Barna has written, "It may be that people who experience genuine, revolutionary spiritual transformation are not those who merely ask Jesus to save them from eternal suffering. Instead, they seek eternal peace with God and embrace a life lens that enables them to think and thus act like Jesus."[6] Jesus provides models and encourages forgiveness. This is a worldview that changes the way you look at others. You don't focus on the dirt. You have the perspective of restoration. This is the only sustainable and healthy way for human beings to coexist.

It is impossible to find a model that diagnoses cultural issues as well as the movement Jesus launched. While politicians often struggle with transactional change, the lifestyle model of Jesus focuses on transformational change. It impacts character. It is based on values. This change is sustainable over time. It is transferable to any culture.

During the century following the death and resurrection of Jesus, there was a serious threat to

> **Politicians struggle with transactional change.**

sustainability of the movement. The values and beliefs of the Roman Empire were polar opposite to those of the Christian movement.

Rome suffered from cultural dissonance that paralleled many of the moral, ethical, and cultural wars being fought today. Sadly, the causative issues often become blurred by the smokescreen of laws, rules,

22

or cultural drift. Many are ignorant of the dangerous results.

If you are discouraged by daily news reports, there is another resource you should use for balance. Get the modern version of the Bible called *The Message*. It was developed by Eugene Peterson. Be sure to read the introduction so you understand: This is not a word-for-word study translation of the Bible. It is a meaning-for-meaning version using modern English words and idioms.

Turn in the New Testament to the letter to the Romans. This letter was written to Jewish Christians who lived in Rome. They were surrounded by Roman culture as it was morally unraveling. You will likely be astounded by the parallels with life today. You may find some critics who call it "fake news." However, historians from all backgrounds, including non-Christians, will tell you Rome was declining from internal moral decay.

Romans was not written by Jesus. It is a cultural treatise by Paul, one of His next-generation leaders. As you read, connect the dots to many of the cultural challenges we face today. Focus on the strategic diagnosis Paul provides for the issues. It is a lesson as fresh as today's *New York Times*.

Here is a real-life compass for those living in a deteriorating culture:

So here's what I want you to do, God helping you:
Take your everyday, ordinary life—your sleeping,
eating, going-to-work, and walking-around life—and
place it before God as an offering. Embracing what
God does for you is the best thing you can do for him.

Don't become so well-adjusted to your culture that you fit into it without even thinking. Instead, fix your attention on God. You'll be changed from the inside out. Readily recognize what he wants from you, and quickly respond to it. Unlike the culture around you, always dragging you down to its level of immaturity, God brings the best out of you, develops well-formed maturity in you.[7]

The followers of Jesus in the first century struggled with civil dissonance, as so many of us do today. Their approach was to embrace the struggle, with God's help. Did it work? Eventually, years later, the Roman emperor Constantine declared the Roman Empire "Christian." While his declaration didn't describe everyone in the empire by any means, civility did improve greatly.

In his book *How Successful People Think*, John Maxwell writes this about the portion of Romans footnoted above:

Romans 12:1-2 describes how God changes our thinking. If you change your thinking, you can change your life. If you change your thinking, you can change your church. If you change the thinking of your church, you can change the world. This is what Jesus was doing every time he taught 'The Kingdom of God is like....'[8]

Jesus proclaimed a culture that is very different.

Increasing Civility

There are two very different approaches to increase civility. The transactional approach says, "We need more laws. Therefore, we need more lawmakers. Therefore, we need more government." The transformational approach says, "We need some laws, of course—and some government. But the most important part of the solution is the transformation of people." This is where faith, education, and rehabilitation are emphasized. The transaction/transformation debate is understood easily through controversies such as gun control. One side says, "We need more laws." The other side says, "We need some laws, but guns don't kill people. People kill people, sometimes with guns." Many would add, "Some guns should be used only by the military."

Consider your own approach to life. Is it *primarily* transactional or transformational? Transactional influence occurs by leverage. Leverage is focused on contracts, laws, and regulations. Transformational influence can be *funneled through* contracts, laws, and regulations but is birthed at a whole different level. Love, respect, purpose, decency, honor, civility—that is what

> **Transformational influence is birthed at a whole different level.**

makes it transformational. These are cultural, character issues. They don't originate in actions. They come from culture. Culture drives character. Character produces civility. Civility determines your actions. No matter how much you yell at your apple tree, make rules about it, spray it, and fertilize it, it won't produce peaches. The fruit of your life is an inside job.

Consider the issue of respect. For many, the lack of respect for leaders today is beyond comprehension. You can observe disrespect in government, business, schools, and churches. Seeds of disrespect mature into crops of civil disobedience. Let's return to how you drive your car.

Do you drive your car following the speed limit? If you do, you are amazed by the vast majority of people who speed right past you. This is no small issue. It is not about miles per hour. It is about disrespect. It's not just disrespect for traffic laws. It's disrespect for the sanctity of life.

The speed limits are provided to protect life: not just yours, but another's life and the children who are in the car with them. So what is the issue behind the issue? We don't have enough law enforcement? We don't have enough money for law enforcement? No! It's not a law enforcement issue. It is a moral issue. Ultimately, it is the value of life, plus the respect for authority. Those are the issues behind the issue.

The level of traffic deaths isn't simply about the lack of law enforcement or the need to build better cars. It is also an issue of people who lack strong moral character. It is evidence of a "me-centered" culture. "My way or the highway." Actually, it's "my way *on* the highway." This translates to every area of life. How does it impact your life?

Jesus' movement focuses on cultural values. Do you know the line, "To love another person is to see the face of God"? This quote, from *Les Misérables*, is a powerful, amazing story of the French Revolution. In this story, a poor man steals an expensive artifact from the church. He is caught, and the officers bring him to the priest. They ask the priest what kind of severe punishment should be given. At this point, the priest, in an amazing act of forgiveness, chooses to say he loaned the man the artifact and no punishment was necessary. Would that kindness impact you?

In *Les Misérables*, the act of forgiveness had enormous influence on the man's life. It amounted to a transformational change: love in the context of a relationship with God. It is in this context that the words take on meaning: "To love another person is to see the face of God."[9] Leadership by transformational change is powerful. When Jesus died on the cross and rose to life three days later, not one newsfeed in Rome picked up the story. It just wasn't Roman Empire news. Yet remember, a few centuries later, Constantine declared the entire empire "Christian." That is why, still today, one of the first branches of Christianity, the Roman Catholic Church, has its headquarters in that city.

Jesus: Civility Personified

Jesus is called by many names: "Son of God," "Savior," "Lamb of God," "Redeemer," "Son of Man," and many more. These are titles you won't find: "Developer of Respect," "Incredible Strategist," "Movement Genius." However, by any measurement, they fit. When it comes to behavior? Jesus is the number one "Restoration Specialist of Civility." Beyond all the spiritual, eternal ramifications, He is the champion of polite, courteous respect and love for people. He lived, and died, to show God's love for the people He created—including you.

Think about it:

    (1) Jesus bypassed symptoms to get to the causative issues of the heart.

(2) He formed a movement of spontaneous regeneration. How does it work?

Without any fanfare, Jesus approached twelve ordinary guys and invited them: "Come follow me." It is doubtful they had any clue what they signed up for. Jesus trained no army, had no weapons, didn't require a college degree, didn't interview for skills, and used no aptitude tests. He had no headquarters, no funding, and no marketing scheme. It is the most unlikely venture to succeed in history. However, he had a unique *strategy* that is counterintuitive in our fast-paced world. You might never consider it, from the position of logistics. It's even challenging to get Christians to do it! It's that unique. Yet, it is still powerful.

Jesus' life personified the Ten Commandments. Beyond that, He had no laws or bylaws. No constitution. He focused on love, forgiveness, restoration, healing, teaching, and empowering twelve guys in a central group and a larger circle of men and women who caught His values, beliefs, attitudes, priorities, and worldviews.

Jesus called the twelve "disciples." Basically, they hung out with him for three years. He told them stories, which some people call "parables." He modeled love for the unlovable: that woman caught in adultery, a despised tax collector, an "untouchable" with leprosy. He did some amazing stuff. He healed people, raised a few people from the dead, walked on water, and fed a large crowd with two fish and five loaves of bread. The real game-changer of His approach is how He led the disciples to become different people. For Jesus, it wasn't about performance. His disciples were not known for what they could do, but—first and foremost—who they were and who they became.

This is the key to a transformational movement: Jesus diagnosed life from a cultural perspective. This culture is called the "Kingdom of God" or the "Kingdom of Heaven." The stories he told summarized a new way to live, a transformative way to impact the world. That was the byproduct.

Jesus' focus teaches a lot about the power of civility, the power of respect. This focus changes the world. It has become a historical watershed for many around the globe. It divided BC and AD. That's quite a mark on history! However, what is insightful for a world like ours is Jesus' approach. It could change everything. It does change everything. It will change you.

An example is a good way to explain how Jesus championed a civil approach. Socrates once said, "Today's children are tyrants. They disobey their parents, gobble their food, and tyrannize their teachers."[10] So, how do you raise kids? There are two fundamentally different approaches, plus a mixture of both. One approach is to lay down the rules. "Finish your dinner, then you can go play." "Brush your teeth; it's time to go to bed." As they get older, the rules get more complicated: "No computer games until you finish your homework." "You can date my daughter, but get her home by 11 p.m."

The rules get piled up over time. The challenge? No one can predict the various bad behavior choices children and young adults can make. You can't anticipate everything. Yet, many parents try...hard.

The same challenges face national governments. No one predicted opioids would become an abused substance. So, the lawmakers had to *react* and form laws to protect people from killing themselves. However, just like parents, no government can legislate morality. No legal, governing body will ever anticipate all the creative ways human beings can harm each other, themselves, and their communities. How do you cope with so many variables?

A great metaphorical story concerning this dilemma can be told about a large company. Delta Airlines is huge. When I investigated their approach a few years ago, they had 80,000 workers, scattered all over the world, working hundreds of different time schedules in dozens of different countries, in numerous languages. It makes a family of four seem simple—which it is not!

Here is what I discovered: There are so many different situations a gate agent or flight attendant might encounter, it is impossible to have a procedure manual (with rules and regulations) that covers them all. Even if they had one, it would take days to read. Of course Delta, like all major airlines, has some non-negotiable regulations that fit everyone. However, beyond those regulations, how can a company cover the millions of potentialities?

> **Recapturing culture leads to restoring civility.**

How can you cover all the possibilities with your kids? How can a civil nation deal with millions of citizens? You do what Delta did. They developed a culture. Their culture is a general framework that sets the tone and direction of all 80,000 workers. This same approach works for families and governments. The challenge is not that the family is too large or the government is too complicated. The real issue is that we often underestimate the value of culture. *Recapturing culture leads to restoring civility.* So, how did Jesus demonstrate culture?

The Christian Movement

If you look at Jewish/Christian history, you recognize a very different leadership approach at different times. You could say it this way: "We are not here to make a difference in the world; we are here to make the world different."[11] The Bible is divided into two periods, the Old Testament and the New Testament. The word "testament" can be translated "covenant." It is like an agreement between God and those people who choose to let Him into their lives.

The Old Testament was a phase of God's interaction with people centered around the Ten Commandments. They were a short version of what God said works best for humans. People show honor, respect, and love to God (like children to parents) by obeying these commandments. Like biological children, God's children aren't perfect, so there are many mishaps along the way. God is loving like a father, forgives His children, and constantly refreshes their memory about the ten "rules."

Meanwhile, to practice this relationship with God, His people made up hundreds of other rules and regulations. It became a nightmare just to remember them. From God's point of view, this was just for a season—a long one—until the new covenant arrived with God's promised deliverer. The New Testament recognizes Him as Jesus. This Jesus reiterated the Ten Commandments as valid. However, like the capacity of many governments and companies, no one could remember everything about what God commanded. Think about our world. Some of the temptations that lead many people to self-destruct today didn't exist two years ago! What will it be like a hundred years from now? Who could guess?

Consequently, Jesus developed a culture—a framework providing a safety net for people to thrive and get along with each other. It's perfect. But it's not. Why? Because people aren't perfect. If you read the stories Jesus told, you recognize the development of culture. Every time Jesus said, "The Kingdom of God is

> **You can't legislate morality.**

like…," He built on this culture. Culture shapes people. Laws only work among those who are shaped. No country, company, family, or person survives on laws alone. Not over the long haul. You can't legislate morality.

Jesus models an approach that goes beyond rules, laws, and regulations. He provides a culture—called the Kingdom of God—for healthy, productive living, no matter what the circumstances. Our world works best with people who are cultural architects. Yet, many people are bogged down, limited to laws and rules. *When people debate or struggle with each other, it is usually because they assume they have a similar cultural viewpoint when, in fact, they don't.*

We need to recognize that we often struggle with cultural clarification. We argue too much about symptoms, yet fail to diagnose the issues behind the issues. So much energy, time, and turmoil exists because we are not communicating our cultural presuppositions. This is true for governmental leaders, parents, company leaders, teachers—everyone!

Jesus taught about a culture built on five elements.[12] Together, they serve as a compass of culture. Here, they are unpacked for clarity:

1. Values—your values are what you consider important. Behind many of the debates, tensions, and struggles, few are asking the value question: "What is really important concerning this issue?"

5 Elements of Culture
1. Values
2. Beliefs
3. Attitudes
4. Priorities
5. Worldviews

2. Beliefs—your beliefs are what you demonstrate is truth. Not everyone agrees about which issues are absolute truth. In discussions about global warming or abortion, who is asking about the truth issue behind the issue? Not everyone agrees about truth, but when you discuss it, you learn from each other. When you know the *why*, you are closer to discovering the *how*…to move forward.

3. Attitudes—your attitude represents your posture or position about the issues behind the issues. Could you ever elect to office a sex offender who committed the crime twenty years ago? The issue behind the issue includes your posture concerning forgiveness and your attitude about the potential of restoration.

4. Priorities—priorities are what you will always do first. If you say you have a priority for exercise, but never exercise, it is actually just a wish or good thought. It is not a priority! What if you are in a debate about school choice? Is your priority a Christian education or a private education, using tax dollars? If you say your priority is Christian education for your children, but rarely worship God yourself, your "priority" may be a smokescreen. Your hypocrisy won't even fool your kids.

5. Worldviews—your worldview reflects how you see the world

and the way the world works. If your worldview says that open borders are impacting the drug trade, you might want to build a wall. If your worldview is that drugs are an issue to be solved by helping those who are addicted, you might want more social programs to treat drug addiction. You may also want more law enforcement to catch drug traffickers. In a complex world, smart people operate with a both/and or "all of the above" approach.

People have different perspectives. That's not the point. The issue is this: How do you process life's challenges? Do you argue, fight, call people names, or attack others? Or can you utilize the five elements of culture to get to the issues behind the issues—and figure it out in a *civilized* approach? If you are willing to dig 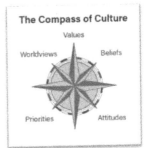 deep, to the level of culture, your approach will uncover the issues behind the issues. Goethe said, "When values are not clear, laws are unenforceable."[13]

So many parents make rules about what they expect from their children. However, they fail to have the cultural discussion that addresses every child's question: "Why?" Sadly, parents miss out on their best parenting: conversations about cultural values, beliefs, attitudes, priorities, and worldviews. They go for the quick fix: "Why? Because I said so!" And the child thinks, "I can't wait to get out of this house."

Companies can fall into the same trap. Their workers know the rules and keep them in order to hang onto their jobs. If it ends there, it might be called "threat management." But what about a situation with a customer that is not covered by the rules? If you have a strong positive culture, workers operate from values and win the admiration of the customer. The company wins, too!

Christian churches aren't immune to drift from their Founder's culture. Church people baptize bylaws, rules, and regulations as sacred. They lose sight of the genius of a movement, the culture of the Kingdom. Many church people know more about the rules than what Jesus taught. The result? Churches implode. They simply move toward incompetence—and decline.

Governments that were once Christian-based drift into a post-Christian malaise. They become tragically distressed. Politicians operate with opposite worldviews. They never get past the symptoms. The dysfunction is a distraction to the way of life and a major discouragement to the populace.

When people can't agree, they become obstructionists. The only way out of that mess is to sit down with mutual respect and ask "Why? Why are you for/against this approach?" Unless the "why" conversation gets to the cultural elements, people remain stuck in the mud of mediocrity. Our world needs

> **When people can't agree, they become obstructionists.**

cultural architects who are driven to the causative issues behind the issues. Otherwise, people talk right past one another.

If you focus on the cultural level, life becomes much healthier. How you get along casts light or darkness on future generations. If it's light—even if you don't agree on everything—the conversation is on a substantive level. Then it becomes constructive conversation because you are operating at the causative level—focused on the issues behind the issues.

Jesus, the master of civility, said something astounding about Himself. He said, "I am the way, the truth, and the life;..."[14] His cultural elements point your way. They empower you to seek the truth. His civil approach generates life. He even promises eternal life. He calls you to spread those truths.

From the wisdom of Jesus, there are seven lessons for civility. In the next chapter we will focus on how culture spreads. Lesson #1 focuses on the tremendous power behind "the infectious principle."

Chapter Three

The Infectious Principle: Lesson #1

"If you don't stand for anything, you'll fall for everything."[1]

If you breathe, if your heart is beating, you are influencing someone. If no one is in the room, you are influencing yourself—by what you think…and by what you edit out of your thoughts. You are contagious— your culture infects others. Do you take seriously how you impact them? *Here is the good news: If you practice respect, it is contagious. It is caught by those around you.*

What do you value? What, for you, is truth? How would you describe your attitude—your posture toward others, life, issues? What are your priorities, those

> **If your heart is beating, you are influencing someone.**

efforts, people, ideas you consistently put first, second, third—before everything else? What is your worldview? How do you see the world? Are you optimistic, or are you a pessimist? Are you hopeful or discouraged? Whether you realize it or not, you are infectious!

Some people see Jesus as their Savior, the Son of God. Others do not. That concept will be debated until the end of time, and then we'll all likely know. Based on historical evidence, it is clear that Jesus is the greatest influencer who ever lived. Up against any other, His movement is the most effective, the most impactful in history. By the numbers, it's infectious.

Jesus' strategy is simple, yet profound. It's not an academic exercise, but a transformative, living *relationship*: (1) Develop in your followers a culture that influences their behavior; a culture that serves as a compass for living; a culture that is clearly articulated and demonstrated by those who believe it; (2) multiply that culture in others by relationally nurturing them to use this compass and clearly articulate it to others.

In this world of human beings, we are often tough on each other, especially when someone makes a bad mistake. A mistake is an *event*. Jesus provided a different view. It is an approach that looks at all human beings *in process*. Everyone makes mistakes. Some mistakes are, in human terms, greater than others. Jesus expressed a different view: All mistakes, all wrongs, are equally terrible. It only takes one, of any size, to be rejected by your Creator.

However, you can ask for forgiveness. Jesus declared that He died to pay for all of your mistakes. This is the "process" view rather than an "event" concept. First and foremost, you are not a human *doing;* you are a human *being.* You are a

> **You are not a human doing; you are a human being.**

person in process. No matter what the mistake, if you are truly sorry and ask for forgiveness, you get it. And other people should accept that. If they don't, they are making a mistake of their own. Jesus taught a prayer that includes, "God, forgive our trespasses (mistakes), as we forgive those who trespass against us." It is a very different culture!

This is the concept of restoration. It grows out of love, respect, and recognition that we all make mistakes—lots of them. Some of the stupid stuff we do as young kids or adults is horrible. However, those

38

mistakes don't have to be permanent, forever tarnishing life. If that were the case, the whole human race would be labeled "losers."

Forgiveness

Asking for forgiveness and forgiving others is a lifestyle of peace. Your compass needle points to hope. Living the perspective of restoration makes civility possible. Why? Nobody's perfect—except for God. No matter what, God has hope for you. No matter what, we should have hope for one another. Can you name anyone who would like all their private indiscretions made public? Then why would anyone ever do that about someone else? Who has that right, except God? Yet, God doesn't have that punitive culture. Therefore, how could you? Why should you?

A few years ago, I met Raymond. He applied to participate in the ten-month spiritual formation adventure for young adults called SEND North America[2]. He was eighteen and living in a homeless shelter. Why? He just got out of prison.

At sixteen, Raymond was a drug lord in Detroit. He was very "successful." He made enough money to own two homes, one in Detroit and one in Los Angeles. Then he got caught. He was sent to prison. A chaplain reached out to him. Raymond gave his life over to God. In time, he became such a changed person, the judge greatly reduced his sentence—an official act of forgiveness. This is a mechanism of civil society—an act of civility. However, his parents rejected him—a rejection of civility. So, Raymond was living in a homeless shelter, accepted by God, rejected by family.

Raymond was interviewed and accepted for the ten-month SEND training for young adults. This is the spirit of civil restoration.

Today? Raymond is part of a team starting a new church in Michigan. Civility gives people a second chance. *Civility looks forward to what you can become, not backward at what you've done.* Restoration generates hope. Hope energizes. It is the ray of sunshine peeking through dark storm clouds. Hope fuels the human spirit—the dawning of a new day.

One of Jesus' followers, Peter, asked, "...how often should I forgive someone who sins against me? Seven times?" Jesus replied, "Seventy times seven."[3] This is a polite way of saying, "Civilized life is a process of restoration. Don't give up on imperfect people. They are all we have. No one is perfect. Hope is never gone." Given the chance, people often rise to the new level of your hopeful expectations. Civilized people allow others to grow. Hope is infectious!

Some "religious" scholars approached Jesus with a challenge. They came with a woman caught in the very act of adulterous sex. In their morally rigid approach, trying to govern unilaterally by laws, the standing rule was that she should be stoned to death on the spot. Given the circumstances, this woman was likely naked in front of the whole village.

> **Civilized life is a process of restoration.**

"So, what do you think," the religious leaders asked Jesus, "can we stone her?" Right! That was the law. He replied, "Sure, anyone among you who is perfect can throw the first rock." The crowd dispersed. No rocks! Jesus said to the woman, "Does no one condemn you?...Neither do I. Go on your way. From now on, don't sin."[4] Legalism is "easy." But human beings have the capacity to forgive and restore. It's a gift, and a responsibility.

This isn't about a society without laws. It's a society mature enough to focus on love, forgiveness, and restoration. This is civil responsibility. We are always looking for the quick fix, but human beings aren't that simple! No one is perfect. We are all on a journey, always learning, continually growing, helping one another along. Legalism without restoration is uncivilized.

So, if a noted country leader is accused and proven to have broken a law as a teenager, does that close the door on their acceptance as a leader several years later? First, if that were true, there would be no leaders. Second, your approach will be based on whether you see life—with mistakes—as a process or an event. In a political race, it's amazing how many television commercials are focused on what is *wrong* with the other candidate. In a civil society, why is that allowed? Why isn't the focus on what is *right* with the candidate the commercial is recommending for office? Everybody wants to take the shortcut, the quick fix. Legalism. Human beings can be better.

The Quick Fix

The natural inclination is to jump at the quick fix. Usually the shortcut becomes the longest path. How does that quick fix appear? Ever hear someone say, "We've always done it that way?" The "same old, same old" requires no thinking, planning, or discomfort. If the world worked well in that approach, you would be riding a horse to work. Good citizens look for the best way, not the familiar way. You don't play fast and loose with your cultural compass, but through that lens, the approach is "whatever works best, now." It's more productive to focus on the doughnut, not the hole.

The quick fix only seems pragmatic: Mold and shape others, using slogans, posters, documents. Change your company, the staff, your children, and your church, using the slogan of the month. The momentary quick fix assures that it will change and improve *nothing* that really matters. Every once in a while, however, a slogan sticks. Why? It has transformational impact!

As mentioned in Chapter One, if you look on the wall behind the podium in the U.S. Congress, you will see a slogan that has triumphed over time. It says, "In God we trust." It's also printed on U.S. currency. Does it signify that everyone operates from the culture it implies? Not a chance! That doesn't make the slogan wrong. Just ineffective. You don't mold culture with a slogan. Yet, the slogan can reflect culture. That slogan was the compass of many of the founding fathers of the U.S. They weren't perfect, by any means. But they were quite clear about certain values, beliefs, attitudes, priorities, and worldviews.

Our house is by a lake. On the lake side of the house is one of my favorite places in the whole world—at least in the summer. It is a porch that overlooks the lake. On the wall of the porch, not far from the outdoor grill, is a slogan I picked up at a store somewhere. It says, "Come, sit on the porch. The drinks are cold and the friendship is free." Will the slogan contribute to anyone's culture? No, but the relationships built on that porch may!

The quick-fix approach plagues busy parents in their fast-paced life of work and raising a family. So, the natural tendency is to "preach" directives to their kids: "Big girls don't do that." "Eat your broccoli; you'll grow up to be big and strong." So, kids grow up in a world of directives: "Do this, don't do that!" Some parents demonstrate a directive for their children saying, "Do as I say, not as I do." Of course, the children grow up and most often do what they saw their parents doing. That is the power of influence—for good, or for bad. You are infectious!

As you influence others, you should watch what you say, but pay very close attention to how you act. Most often, someone is watching! You are molding others through your influence, what you say and what you don't. You shape culture by what you do and what you

> **You are a mind molder.**

neglect. In the power of influence, you are a mind molder—for good or for bad.

It seems that plant managers like to put clever statements on the cafeteria walls. When I worked at Ford Motor Company in the parts depot, the banner read, "A fair day's work for a fair day's pay." My work ethic had already been established before I got that job. I worked hard and fast, and I enjoyed it. It was my culture. Where did I learn it? From my grandparents, my parents, Miss Dorian (my ninth grade English teacher, also known by many of the students as "the witch"), my football coach, and my pastor. These people all worked hard and worked me hard. The banner at Ford? I thought, "Everyone knows that: 'A fair day's work for a fair day's pay.'" (I was young and naïve.)

Pastors and priests preach. Military leaders bark orders and yell at subordinates. Politicians look for media sound bites. CEOs give pep

> **Culture is more about who you are...and who you become.**

talks. But it's not just about what you say. The power to change culture is more about who you are...and who you become. That is really how you become culture-contagious!

Culture: More Caught Than Taught

Jesus modeled life before his twelve disciples—for three years! He lived and demonstrated the culture. He wanted them to catch it and pass it on. Changing culture is more than a program. It is a way of life. Leo Tolstoy said, "Everyone thinks of changing the world, but no one thinks of changing himself."[5] Your world, your little portion of the planet, changes one person at a time. It occurs by the infectious principle.

Epidemiology is the study of the spread of infectious diseases. You may remember Chuck Colson. He was a Washington politician caught in the Watergate scandal during the Nixon administration. He went to prison.

> **Culture: People catch it when you get up close and personal.**

However, while there, someone introduced him to Jesus. It changed his life. By the time he was released from prison, he had learned how to deal with the systemic challenges of our society. He had discovered the way to effectively produce change.

A friend of mine, Jim Manthei, told me what he heard Colson say at a business luncheon, "Some people say that Christianity has not really had an effect on changing things in society. However, Christianity is sort of like the Asian flu. You can read the productivity scales of the country, and when the Asian flu appears, say on the West Coast, all of a sudden the productivity scales show a decrease. Then, pretty soon, you find it spreading to the Midwest—and finally to the East. And yet, the Asian flu only moves from one person to another at a time. However, it has tremendous effects on society. In the same way, Christianity moves through a culture, one person at a time, and has tremendous overall effects."

We are all infectious in one way or another. If you want to be

> **We are all infectious in one way or another.**

a positive influencer, move beyond the quick fix. "Infect" those you influence with a respectful culture. Think about how this could bring profit to your business, greater effectiveness to Congress, spiritual growth to your church, a quality of life to your kids, peace to your community, harmony to the sports team you coach, and sanity to the nation. As you live your life, make sure you follow the infectious principle: Get up close and personal with others, and let them catch culture from you. Christian leader Howard Hendricks says, "You can impress people at a distance, but you can impact them only close up."[6]

If you have the flu, quarantine yourself. If you have caught the culture that can improve our world, spend your time with people. Model your culture. They catch it when you get up close and personal. You are never a movement of one. You are an influencer of many who become influencers of multitudes.

Think about what the Apostle Paul wrote to the people at Corinth. You need to know: Corinth was known as one of the most corrupt rat holes of the Mediterranean region at the time. He wrote:

The world is unprincipled. It's dog-eat-dog out there!
The world doesn't fight fair. But we don't live or fight

our battles that way—never have and never will. The tools of our trade aren't for marketing or manipulation, but they are for demolishing that entire massively corrupt culture. We use our powerful God-tools for smashing warped philosophies, tearing down barriers erected against the truth of God, fitting every loose thought and emotion and impulse into the structure of life shaped by Christ.[7]

The Infectious Movement

Jesus' marching orders to His followers are directed to change the world, one person at a time. David Gurgen said, "If you want to go fast, go alone. If you want to go far, go together."[8] Jesus spent three years kindling a fire that has lasted 21 centuries. It is now present in every country, every culture, representing billions of people. If His impact doesn't catch your attention, ask someone to take you to the morgue!

How did Jesus do it? How did He do it in three years? It's no secret, but most people don't get it—even many preachers, who should know better. Most of us have the inclination to *go big and move fast*. Jesus did just the opposite. I know, it doesn't seem to

> **Start small and go slow.**

make sense. That's why so many people miss it. Jesus' approach was to *start small and go slow*.

Jesus gathered those twelve disciples and spent three years with them. Even when He went to public gatherings, like a wedding, they were with Him. It may be why, when they ran out of wine as the story goes, Jesus made more, from water! I wonder if the disciples thought,

"Who wouldn't follow Him?" When you are up close and personal with others, you mold the culture of civility—by what you say, how you act, what you do, how you react—by who you are. Remember, respect for others is caught more than taught.

Jesus continually used the metaphor, "The Kingdom of God," as mentioned earlier. As He told stories, He began, "The Kingdom of God is like…." Once in a while He would say, "My Kingdom is not like this world," not of this world. In these stories, Jesus would lay out a different set of values, beliefs, attitudes, priorities, and worldviews—a very different culture. A unique culture. During "downtime" around the campfire or a meal, Jesus' disciples would ask questions. There were discussions as they processed this new culture. Interaction is an important element of culture building. It can't be all one way, top-down—even though it begins from the influencer to the followers.

Many politicians argue. Good politicians, those who are cultural architects, have a conversation.

> **Good politicians are cultural architects.**

Some politicians favor the podium, the cameras, the sound bites. Yet, they stonewall conversations. They should never be reelected. Dictatorial parents bark rules. Cultural parents discuss and model values with their children. Some people pull rank to "get it done" fast. Some people vote to get the win. However, cultural architects dig deep to understand. They listen as well as talk. Their goal is to get to bedrock cultural assumptions. They model their cultural commitments. They invest in others.

Jesus modeled culture: preaching in public, challenging the religious leaders from the old school, healing sick people, even casting out demons—which really gets your attention! Then the disciples and their leader would get away by themselves in woods, a garden, or a boat, discuss what happened, and ask questions. The process continued. This is the process of enculturation. There are no shortcuts!

You can infect respect by telling stories. You can share, discuss, and model the cultural distinctives: what is important, what you believe, your attitude, priorities, and worldviews. If you are a parent influencing your children, you probably won't use Jesus' words, "My Kingdom is like...." What you are sharing is something like, "I've discovered, in life, this works for me...."

In history, there have been major companies, great nations, whole civilizations, and great families that have experienced dramatic prosperity, followed by severe implosion. The rise and fall of these giants has almost always been due to cultural drift. A generation fell into civil disobedience—perhaps several generations. The pain and loss injures many people. Cultural drift kills

> **Cultural drift kills countries.**

companies, families, churches, and sports teams. It kills countries. This is the infectious principle in reverse. Skip one or two generations of respectful and polite culture—and you lose it all.

Rebuilding culture takes time and discipline. This is why, perhaps, so many fail by taking the quick-fix route. However, nothing develops productivity and sustains effectiveness like culture. The shortcut is to focus on *methods*. But methods are not what make you great. Methods change. If they don't, you go out of business, experience political gridlock, develop a church that is no longer contextualized to your audience, or raise kids who are not equipped for their own generation.

Principles, on the other hand, are firm and solid. They transcend time, age groups, technological changes, and fads. Your culture is your foundation. Everything else is up for grabs! *"Methods are many; principles are few. Methods always change; principles never do."*[9]

Examples of methodological change are everywhere. Henry Ford said, "Any customer can have a car painted any color that he wants so long as it is black."[10] Obviously, that changed! But it didn't change the culture of how Ford builds quality cars. Painting every car black is a focus on method. Quality products come from a work ethic culture.

> **Methods are many; principles are few. Methods always change; principles never do.**

Infectious Communication

In 2017, a new U.S. President, Donald Trump, at 70 years old (!), created a communication change of major proportions: He communicated directly to constituents (and others) using Twitter. This methodological change enthralled some and outraged others. Twitter was actually invented years before and used by millions of people. However, the impact on the "power" of the press was enormous! It was an example of a method that changed the culture...of the press. It communicated the culture of the president to the people without a filter. It became contagious communication. Like it or hate it, the presidential use of Twitter is transformative.

Some churches occasionally use words no longer active in contemporary English language. Words like "thee" and "thou" are not more "holy" than "you" and "your." However, they send an antithetical message that Christians don't profess: "God is old or out of date." Words represent the packaging of meaning. They are a medium. But the medium communicates an infectious message as well.

At one time, Episcopalian, Methodist, Lutheran, and Baptist were brand names that meant something. Now, not so much. Whether it's good or bad, right or wrong, it's a fact! This is one of many reasons nondenominational churches are growing while many denominational congregations are declining. Unwillingness to change methods even kills churches. The real shock? Some actually believe some methods, like dress codes for clergy, old-language songs, and liturgical styles from the Middle Ages are actually principles!

Some years ago, I taught hundreds of missionaries at a conference held in Almaty, Kazakhstan, near the western border of China. I asked one of the missionary pastors, "What denomination are you with?" He said, "When you're on a mission field, you can't afford to be in competition with each other. We are all Christians, and we help each other succeed." Your mission forms your communication.

The Internet, television, and films all contribute to cast the mold for future generations. They communicate in ways that shape culture. These "civil filters" shape behavior and norms more than most would like to admit. They absolutely are a factor for shaping civilization, in both positive and negative directions. They impact the future of civilization, one person at a time.

Symbols are pictures that communicate culture. Think about efforts that have come and gone. Cathedrals in Europe? Tourist attractions. The Roman Empire? Gone except for a few aging relics.

Fortune 500 companies of 50 years ago? Gone or greatly changed. However, the basic movement Jesus began, while constantly changing methods, keeps the principles. It is still moving twenty centuries later, influencing billions of people. The effort to develop culture provides sustainability! Culture is infectious.

Are you a cultural architect? If so, you likely contribute to the sustainability of multigenerational families, businesses, universities, sports franchises, firefighters, airlines, churches, and governments. You focus on cultural values, beliefs, attitudes, priorities, and worldviews. These elements provide sustainability. Why? People catch them! **Are you a cultural architect?** Departure from them signals doom. Focus on methods as if they are unchangeable, and you invite obsolescence and self-destruction. Adaptability of methods provides sustainability. This is why our world desperately needs cultural architects who reestablish civility!

Multiplying the Culture

How do you multiply the culture? How did Jesus embed the culture to make sure it would multiply? What did He do to assure it would continue for hundreds of years in thousands of cultures, in a wide variety of languages? How did the movement Jesus birthed with twelve keep the culture in the decades that immediately followed? The movement grew rapidly, from twelve to one hundred twenty, to three thousand, to five thousand, to multitudes within decades. How do you keep what is valuable about your culture? This is the greatest challenge.

The culture Jesus built became the DNA of the growing organism—a movement. Jesus did far more than enculturate twelve

> **The culture Jesus built became the DNA of the growing organism.**

disciples. How? Those disciples became *disciplers*. This is the infectious principle. Multiplication was part of their DNA. Growth was a centerpiece of their culture. In fact, when Jesus commissioned them, He didn't say, "Go collect church members." He said, "Go and make disciples."[11]

When we consult churches, we interview a cross section of the members. Frequently, I'm interviewing a couple who have adult children. These couples are active in their church, so I ask about their children. Sadly, more often than not, they report that their children do not attend a church and, therefore, neither do their grandchildren. The faith that is a big part of the parents' life was not *caught* by their kids. The spiritual culture was lost. Why? In most cases, they say they took their children to church, put them in Sunday school, and encouraged them to be in the church's youth group. Sadly, however, they relied solely on the *church*, as an institution, to be the conduit through which their children caught the movement called Christianity.

What did they miss? The parents never *personally* talked to their children about their cultural value of faith. They didn't know that kids don't catch the culture of God's Kingdom from an institution—not even the church. The Christian faith is a personal culture that needs to be discussed relationally, beyond the institution. *This is the infectious principle—you "get it" through up close and personal contact over a long period of time.* It's a relational process, not institutional. It doesn't guarantee the next generation will catch it. However, it greatly increases the likelihood it will stick.

Multiplying culture makes Christianity a movement. The

Christian movement is growing. Wherever it has been lost, it is because the movement has stalled. To be honest, one of those stalled situations includes

> **The infectious principle is a relational, not institutional, process.**

many (but not all) of the churches in North America. Church leaders, and some pastors, are fixated on the crowd. However, no one, not even Jesus, can disciple the crowd. It is impossible to take large numbers of people and relationally disciple them to become disciplers. Preaching doesn't do it. Preaching nourishes people who are already living as active disciples, those who have already been enculturated.

Discipling is, by definition, a relational activity. It's not rocket science. Discipling has several stages: (1) Come close, hang out with me; (2) I do/you watch; (3) I do/you help; (4) You do/I help; (5) You do/I watch; (6) We both follow this process with someone else, or a small group. Building culture must begin with a relational setting. And yes, it could take up to three years. I know this personally.

When it came time for me to give up the reins as leader of Church Doctor Ministries, I discipled Tracee—for three years, as my major focus. Afterward, I continue as an occasional discipler, whenever she requests. Individuals from all over the world have heard Tracee speak. Among those who also have heard me, the common response is, "When we hear Tracee teach, she sounds just like Kent." That's the point! It is not an ego trip for me. It is the power of the discipleship process. Your work lives on! Your work is multiplied! Culture is infectious!

Using the infectious principle, you *invest* in people. *Using* people doesn't cut it. Lecturing others isn't enough. Your greatest objective as a parent is to relationally invest in your children. If you are a principal of a school, you must relationally invest in your teachers—or they may not invest in their students. Good coaches relationally invest in their players. Great leaders relationally connect with their constituents. *This is how culture is caught.*

The relational platform is a genuine 100 percent commitment to listen and speak about cultural ingredients: what is important; what is true; our posture toward others; what we believe are non-negotiables and the way we understand the world and the way it works. *You are building and sharing a compass.*

The development of the few is never complete until they live the culture of developing others. This gives birth, as mentioned earlier, to the law of geometric progression: the genius of Jesus' movement. One person pours life and culture into others, making sure the culture includes the next step: Go and do this with others. This will never occur in a large group. Like the flu, to catch it, you must get up close and personal, transparent and vulnerable. With the non-negotiable commitment to multiply yourself, you develop multipliers who will multiply others. This is the flywheel effect. It starts small and requires time. It is entirely relational. Cultural DNA is not taught but caught. It occurs when you become culturally infectious.

When you multiply your cultural DNA among, say, five people, it takes a long time. However, what happens if, over the following two, three, or four years, you do the same with five more, while the original five each do the same, with five more? You, the one, become five more, equaling six. You take on five more; they take on five each. You have five, but the five have twenty-five, collectively. Now there are twenty-six, plus the original five. Take this progression to three more levels, and the numbers will astound you! You can influence civility in a movement that renews a nation.

Now you have a movement of contagious multiplication of the culture that makes you, your family, your company, your school, your university, your politicians, and your country—*really great.* "Never doubt that a small group of thoughtful committed people can change the world—indeed it's the only thing that ever has!"[12]

> **You have a movement of contagious multiplication.**

You don't have to settle for success. You can reach for significance. This is the exciting worldview discussed in the next chapter. It is the second lesson: success isn't everything. Effectiveness makes you a world changer.

Chapter Four
Don't Settle for Success: Lesson #2

"This is the true joy in life, being used for a purpose recognized by yourself as a mighty one; being a force of nature instead of a feverish selfish little clod of ailments and grievances complaining that the world will not devote itself to making you happy. I want to be thoroughly used up when I die, for the harder I work the more I live. I rejoice in life for its own sake. Life is no 'brief candle' to me. It is a sort of splendid torch which I have got hold of for the moment, and I want to make it burn as brightly as possible before handing it on to future generations."

—George Bernard Shaw[1]

Embedded deep within every individual is the desire to produce and reproduce, to observe some measure of success, and to experience some level of achievement. What about you? What is your end game? Pay off the mortgage? Retirement? A cruise? They are all great goals. However, what is your legacy objective? *Success* is great. Raising kids who are successful and multiply themselves is awesome. What in life, for you, has lasting *significance*—beyond success? Rusty Rustenbach has pointed out, "You and I live in an age when only a rare minority of individuals desire to spend their lives in pursuit of objectives which are bigger than they are. In our age, for most people, when they die it will be as though they never lived."[2]

If you move from beyond success to significance, you will leave civil disobedience behind. You will no longer radiate heat. You will shine like light and brighten the world for everyone.

When I was in high school, nearly all of my classmates wanted to go to college. It was largely a worldview promoted by our parents. If we asked our parents, "Why? Why should I go to college?" the answer was almost always the same: "Money. You'll make more money." While that response is likely accurate, few asked the deeper question: "Why? Why is more money important?" It presupposes the answer, "So you can buy more." Which raises another question, "Why do we need more?" The presupposition is that more stuff makes you—what—happy? That assumption is not demonstrated in real life. For many, however, it is the measure of success. So, what lights your fire?

In this journey we call life, it is easy to believe "success" is the ultimate objective. Yet, a lot depends on how you define success. Many would agree that success is related to status and material wealth. Unfortunately, fewer people give much thought to success as a step in the greater journey: success that leads to significance.

Many describe success as related to stuff. However, significance is usually related to people and to achievements

> **Aim for success that leads to significance.**

considered beneficial to others. If you tell people about your achievements, they are impressed. However, if you also talk about your failures and what you have learned, it impacts them even more. Why? You help them avoid making your mistakes. What is the benefit? You give them the priceless gift of momentum. *Momentum is an engine for movement.* Will people, will the world, be any better because you were here? Have you ever tasted the indescribable fulfillment of contributing beyond the grave?

Have you ever considered this? Success is measured by how much you have. Significance is measured by how much you give. Rick Warren says, "What matters is not the *duration* of your life, but the *donation* of it. Not *how long* you lived, but *how* you lived."[3] When many people talk about success, it's usually about how much they have accumulated. When they talk about significance, it's based on how much they have given. It's like the man who asked the CEO of a manufacturing plant, "In your company, what do you build?" The man replied, "People."

How does this relate to battles we see every day—reflections of diminished civility? Are you focused on fighting for something you love? Or are you focusing on fighting for what you are against? Can you even count the number of protests you've seen on the news in the last year? Of course, it's a human *right* to protest, right? What do those same people do to contribute to the solution? And why doesn't that make the news?

> **Significance is measured by how much you give.**

The movement level of significance is measured by sustainability and replication. Sustainability means you have invested your life in something that will outlast you. Replication refers to your willingness, even joy, to see others duplicate your life achievement beyond your life. It reflects impact on another level, one you personally never achieved.

Previously, I mentioned that I discipled Tracee as the next leader of the church consulting service I birthed, Church Doctor Ministries.

Sometimes people ask me, "How do you feel about the one you trained, who is now your boss?" Honestly, I love it! Sure, she doesn't have the depth of experience I've had in consulting, teaching, and writing. How could she? But that will come—and it's coming quickly. Why? She stands on my shoulders. She can

> **Movement is measured by sustainability and replication.**

learn from and avoid my many mistakes. Church Doctor Ministries is better. But this is the movement level: The ministry will be even stronger at helping churches that will be better at changing lives of people I will never meet in my lifetime. That is a movement!

I also love Tracee's leadership because she has brought greater skills from her business background. I marvel at how she has broken the ceiling of achievement that I built. She has brought so much more that she will, in turn, invest in others. I don't know if our board or staff realize it yet, but she represents validation for what I have invested in the work. She is the embodiment of my life's greatest contribution: a service that lives at the level of sustainability. Is this the objective of your life? I agree with my friend Tom Manthei, who said, "True significance is using your God-given abilities for an eternal purpose."[4]

Success is "What have I done for myself?" *Significance* is "What have I done for others?" *Movement* is "What have I done that is sustainable and expandable?" *Legacy* is "What have I done that lives on in perpetuity?" This dimension of civility moves beyond the concept of success. In this way, civility multiplies respect and invests in civilization among those I will never meet this side of eternity. Change your worldview to this level, and it will light a fire in your soul.

Sustainable Significance

> Legacy is "What have I
> done that lives on in
> perpetuity?"

Jesus is truly the Master, because His movement provides significance that is sustainable, with a lifespan of more than twenty-one centuries. Impressive! He built a culture that changes people, who change others, who change the world. And it grows by exponential multiplication!

Think about it this way, and apply it to your life: It takes one apple seed to grow an apple tree. As it matures, the tree produces numerous apples—*every year*! Many of the seeds from these apples—perhaps thousands—lay on the ground, and eventually other apple trees grow to produce more apples with more seeds. This is an apple tree movement. This is the power of God's creation. If you value life, invest yourself in efforts that multiply *and* outlive you.

Your greatest contribution is to exercise influence to the level of a movement. Getting kids through college? Not enough! Seeing preschool kids learn their alphabet and go on to kindergarten? Not enough! Making a fortune? Not enough! Becoming a movie star? Not enough! Leading a nation? Not enough!

Do you look at your occupation and say, "This is what I do; this is who I am"? Does what you do define you? Is it your focus to achieve success? Or, is your ultimate goal significance? Do you get up in the morning to make a difference? This is the challenge: make a difference in what? Your paycheck? Your car payments?

Real significance always occurs when you make a difference in *people*. John Wesley, a Christian leader of the eighteenth century, said, "Do all the good you can, by all the means you can, in all the places you can, at all the times you can, to all the people you can, as long as ever you can."[5] No matter who you are or what you do: You have influence in the lives of people. What are you doing to grow them? To help them? To serve them? To encourage them? To love them? Do you think this worldview would increase the climate of civility in our world? It's a matter of motive. It's in your soul. It defines who you really *are*, far beyond whatever you *do*.

Jesus developed a never-ending movement of exponential multiplication. He didn't have a corner office, not even a building. He didn't build an organization, not even a church. He built people. And they built churches—by the millions—and touched the lives of others, by the billions. The fuel? Love. Love for people. It sounds so simple. Too elementary. The entire movement is built on a foundation of these three words: "God is love."[6] It is followed by these words, "We love because He first loved us."[7] To many, it sounds simplistic. For those who get it, it works. It is the bedrock of civility.

Life is never perfect. Some people blame God. They get it wrong. It's not perfect because people aren't perfect. But God's love includes the precious and powerful gift of forgiveness. The dynamic of forgiveness moves the compass needle so much closer to civility.

> **Forgiveness moves the compass needle so much closer to civility.**

Beyond the Bottom Line

You can live beyond the bottom line. Adjust your culture: values, beliefs, attitudes, priorities, and worldviews. As a parent, is your endgame raising children who leave the home, equipped for life, a job, and a family? Think beyond: What investment can you make in your children? What values could you instill in them that would improve the lives of those great-great-great-grandchildren you will never meet in your lifetime? What beliefs can you seed into their lives that become a holy infection they will give to friends you will never know? What attitudes will you nurture in your children that may be more valuable than a PhD? What priorities do you demonstrate that might be *caught* by your children, even though you never *taught* them? What worldviews do you represent that may influence your children, impacting their careers long after you are retired?

When you focus on culture, you live a slice of your own legacy before you die. The seeds you plant

> **Focus on culture… the seeds you plant bear fruit for generations.**

bear fruit for generations—just like the apple seeds. This is the difference between success and significance. Building culture in others is your greatest contribution!

Do you ever pray? Whether it's part of your lifestyle or not, do it anyway. Pray: "God, give me the vision, the wisdom, the culture, to plan *now* to become a good ancestor." Spoiler alert: If God answers your prayer and you are wise enough to listen, *be prepared to become a person you never dreamed you could be.* I know, it sounds too simple. But God changes this world, one person at a time. And in the time you read this paragraph, it most likely happened to a thousand people, worldwide.

Live the multigenerational legacy. Don't buy into the insane idea of "living in the moment." If everyone did that, the human race would have self-destructed centuries ago. The legacy of generations signifies you have more influence on people born 200 years from now than you can imagine. Your name may be forgotten. Yet, it's not about you. Your influence will be part of a world you will never see. Plan now for then, so they will be glad you lived—without even knowing "why." And, they may not ever know "who." Think centuries beyond your lifetime.

When I first learned about legacy thinking, I read a statement by Elton Trueblood: "We have made at least a start in discovering the meaning of human life when we plant shade trees under which we know full well we will never sit."[8] I always liked trees. When I was eighteen, Dutch elm disease hit southeast Michigan where I lived. Big, beautiful elm trees were everyone's favorite shade trees. Most people had one or more in their yards. Sadly, the disease killed them by the thousands.

In what turned out to be a futile attempt to stop the spread of the disease, the state of Michigan sent workers who marked the trees with large red tags. The tags read, "You have ten days to remove this tree or you will be fined." Tree removal companies were swamped with work. I saw an opportunity. I purchased some chainsaws, ropes, and a forestry climbing belt and spurs and taught myself how to climb. I hired a few friends. Dead trees provided the money we needed for college. Yet, that wasn't my first connection with trees.

A few years earlier, when I was around ten years old, my parents took me on vacation to join their friends, Tony and Jackie Simpson, at their cabin in northern Michigan. They built the cabin in a wooded area. There was an open field nearby. They hired someone to plant pine trees in that field. Every time we visited them, year after year, the trees had grown larger and larger, without any effort on the part of anyone. I thought: What a great investment!

These tree-related experiences impacted my life. It was sad to see the dead elms removed. But the people desperately needed to get rid of them. The growing pines by the cabin in northern Michigan, once planted, became a young forest without any additional effort. It completely changed the beauty of that cabin location. It planted a seed in me: a love for trees!

Years later, my wife and I moved to Indiana. It was the mid-80s, when America went through a major change in the Farm Bill. The government could no longer pay financial commodity subsidies for corn, wheat, and soybeans. Many farmers went out of business. The family farms made it through, but the "hobby farmers" who were "milking the government" couldn't make payments on marginal properties they bought and rented to "custom farmers." Without the government price support, many "hobby farmers" could not make their payments to the bank. They sold their properties at deflated prices.

We bought one of those properties—144 acres of somewhat awful farm ground: hilly, erodible, piecemeal fields, and swamps. The price was incredibly inexpensive in that moment of opportunity. Some local farmer friends told me it was "a good price, but terrible ground." They were thinking about corn and soybeans. My father-in-law, Ralph, and I were thinking about trees.

My wife, Janet, grew up on Ralph's farm and could outwork most men. She taught preschool, but on spring break, she and I planted trees. We planted, by hand, for nine days, no matter what the weather, year after year. Fast-forward to today. We have planted 62,000 choice hardwood trees grown from seedlings. They now represent a young forest.

It's a legacy project. The day we planted that first tree, we knew we would never see it harvested in our lifetimes. Our two children, and now their spouses, are the trustees after we are gone. It is a certified tree farm, which means it is sustainable. For every tree harvested, at least one more must be planted—forever! What about the proceeds from the sale? The trust we prepared with our attorney says our children own it after we're gone. When they sell timber from the trees, half of the proceeds will be given to Christian missions—forever. The other half of the income can go to expanding the farm and planting more trees.

So, what is my exercise routine and hobby? Pruning trees for quality timber! Over time, we built a house and made some lakes, and now we live in the middle of what is, for us, a paradise! Wildlife is everywhere, and God continues to grow the trees, even while I'm traveling the world helping Christian leaders and churches.

This legacy project is not for everyone. It may not be something you would find fulfilling. That's not the point. What is yours? For us, it's not about trees anyway. It's about helping effective churches change lives. Yes, the trees are doing their part for cleaner air and water, but people matter most. It's an investment to make the world a better place. It's a civility project.

> **Legacy thinking points you to potential for vision and sustainability.**

My point? Legacy thinking through the cultural compass points you to potential for vision and sustainability. Life by values, beliefs, attitudes, priorities, and worldviews provides new horizons you might otherwise never consider. What is your vision? What will you invest in this world for hundreds of years after you die? Don't settle for success. Don't limit your life contributions to the years you spend on this earth. This is the opposite approach to the saying, "Life's too short." You can leave behind more than you ever had while you were here. The Bible even says that when you have life with God, people of all ages will have visions and dreams.[9]

My friend, Ben, is a successful businessman in Michigan. He says, "Success is the reward you gain from being very good at what you do. Significance is using your success to make a difference for eternity. True significance is not what you do for God, but your ability to allow God to accomplish His goals through you."[10]

Life gets hectic. Have you ever taken time off to review your place in history? Not just your history and your lifespan, but legacy thinking: what can "uniquely you" contribute long after you are forgotten? Where you work, what is your ultimate objective? The fiscal bottom line? Or, is it to help build a culture that impacts the lives of your fellow workers, their children, and their grandchildren? Is it to help influence a culture that builds respect in others, who will make a sustainable mark on others? Don't make it all about money! Anybody can do that.

If you are a teacher, is your goal to produce educated graduates? Every school does that. Or is it your objective to develop students who are world changers? Consider your influence—for good or bad. Put your life's work with aspiring students in the backdrop of your country and our world. How is your so-called civilized nation performing—on any scale of social health and vitality? What about the life contentment scale compared to the shocking rise in suicides, shootings, and drug abuse? Are you missing opportunities?

If you are a politician at some level of government, are you content to battle party loyalties to get votes to keep your job in the next election? Or are you a world changer who understands that you are less important than building a culture of love and respect? Is more of your energy invested toward being against the other party, or, are you focused on a culture where transparency rules? How often is discussion focused on learning and developing values, beliefs, attitudes, priorities, and worldviews among fellow politicians and your constituents? Do you have any idea how important that is? "You can't do much about the length of your life, but you can do something about its width and depth."[11] Is that your worldview, your focus? Will your commitment to civilization be so strong that it breaks the undignified gridlock? What is your legacy?

The Jesus Model

Jesus developed followers. As a by-product of their DNA, they developed other followers, who caught the culture of multiplication. No matter who you are or what you do, who are you developing? Mentoring? Apprenticing? No matter what you make, sell, or buy, or how you serve, as you do it, who are you growing—to do it better than you, better for our world?

A "soundbite" of opinionated rhetoric doesn't make you a great person. Nor does your post on Facebook. Truly great people are great diagnosticians—and listeners. Civil

> **Truly great people are great diagnosticians.**

people are learners. Their objective is to sort out the issues behind the issues. They go down in history as cultural architects. They become our heroes. Could that be you?

Everyone must deal with politics of some sort: moms and dads, teachers and preachers, police officers and firefighters, doctors and lawyers. It's part of life everywhere. The word "politics," from Latin and Greek, is related to the word "polite," as mentioned earlier. Imagine that! The primary meaning of "polite" is "having or showing culture" or "good taste." In the Greek, "politics" is defined as having practical wisdom, being prudent and diplomatic. Only in the evolutionary use of the term has it come to mean "crafty" and "unscrupulous." That is compass confusion. Can you get back to the basics?

Who are you developing to "catch" what can't be taught? With whom are you clearly sharing your cultural values, beliefs, attitudes, priorities, and worldviews? If you died tomorrow, would someone be ready to step into your role and do it better—thanks to you? Do you treat people like they *produce something*, or are you focused on the objective that they *become someone*?

Our world is changing, and the rate of change is accelerating. Access to technology allows those lacking transformational culture to create a cesspool of criticism, void of integrity. Many are disrespectful. They have lost their compass of decency. They are tolerated under the banner of "free speech." They are destructive polluters of the human family. They cloud the atmosphere with toxic behavior. It is possible to disagree without being disagreeable. You can have different points of view without being disrespectful. You can be civilized. You can be civil. Respect is within reach.

Lessons from Paul, the Apostle

Paul is the man who wrote a good portion of the New Testament. He was originally a cantankerous, mean-spirited, angry Jewish leader. He actually became a political persecutor of young Christians. He was a brilliant leader with a vicious disposition. He met Jesus in an extraordinary way while traveling to Damascus. His culture was dramatically rearranged. His life changed from success to significance.

Paul wrote numerous letters to "correct" cultural drift among young Christians. He had the same two choices as every parent, boss, teacher, politician, and anyone who ever lived. He could beat them up. (His former life demonstrated he could be mean!) Or, he could challenge and encourage. With a changed culture, he demonstrated a different approach. I call it the "sandwich approach."

Paul began his letters and his speeches with truthful, positive comments about his audience. Then, he focused on correcting their cultural drift—even some touchy behavioral drift. However, he always ended with

> **Sandwich approach:**
> **Begin with praise,**
> **provide correction,**
> **end with praise.**

praise and expressed love and appreciation. That's the sandwich: begin with praise, provide correction, and end with praise. Is that what you do? Today our world is saturated with disruptive dissonance. Try Paul's sandwich. It's a practical step toward cultural reengineering.

Adapting to Change

The disruptive lack of civility and civilized respect, coupled with the speed of information processing, makes it difficult to be adaptive in this rapidly changing world. Adaptive culture-based "civilians" play a vital

> **The key elements for effective adaptive leadership: (1) healthy relationships and (2) trust.**

role in this environment. Adaptive leaders have the potential to move beyond success to significance. The key elements for effective adaptive leadership are: (1) healthy relationships and (2) trust. When you have a clear cultural framework, you can make good choices based on an unclouded, unbiased diagnosis. This is not new. We can learn it from the past.

The U.S. expanded in the early days of settlers with wagon trains. Whole families migrated toward the plains and to the West. The country turned to building an infrastructure system of railroads. That was a great success. However, it appears that those who developed the railroads didn't think through their core purpose. Based on their actions, they defined their business, and their purpose, as railroads. What has been the impact? This is a cultural issue of worldview. Were the builders of railroads focused on transaction or transformation? Money or meaning? The immediate or legacy? Your cultural worldview expands your horizons. Don't settle for success.

For years, if you lived in northern Indiana and wanted to fly out of O'Hare Airport in Chicago, you could take the train to Chicago. However, it didn't connect (until quite recently) with the airport. Chicago has had commuter rail transportation for years, but it didn't connect, for a long time, with the railroad or the airport. This is the point: If railroad builders would have defined their legacy as "transportation," they would likely own, run, or at least connect with the airports—like most of Europe. Railroads were a success, but the builders missed significance.

As the U.S. seeks to improve infrastructure now, this is the question: Will government leaders use the legacy compass? If you operate from a cultural lens, you become adaptable to change and more focused on the big picture. It's easy to get stuck in a narrow worldview as the world rapidly changes. Are you focused on transacting or transforming? Is your endgame focused on success or significance? It's a legacy issue. Do you live your life seeing the big picture? Respect for others broadens your horizons.

You can see this approach in the complicated world Jesus entered. He wasn't limited to the concept of achievement. He developed a culture that led people to become transformed: They became different people! Different people, with an intentional cultural platform, can adapt to challenging changes in the environment. The followers of Jesus were stunned when He was crucified, and many were stunned again when He appeared to hundreds in a resurrected body! The resurrection was a legacy statement: "Even though He died, He lives!"

Jesus' followers adapted because they bought into His culture. A few of the Jewish leaders accepted the change. However, most didn't focus on the culture and couldn't make the change. They were too focused on laws, rules, and "the way we've always done it." So, they killed Jesus! They engineered political stress on the local Roman governor who, under pressure, agreed for Him to be crucified. They never dreamed He would come back from the grave. They were "successful" for three days. But on Easter morning, they realized they missed significance.

71

Adaptive Renewal

You know what's sad? Many churches today are declining because the people get the message but missed the culture. They cling to the teaching but can't adapt to new delivery systems. They place their

> **Adaptive Renewal: Cling to the teaching, but adapt to new delivery systems.**

belief in forms. It's transactional faith. Even Jesus' followers can get stuck in the rut of *religion* and miss the legacy of *faith*.

The cultural compass transforms the way people act and react. They are changed. The Apostle Paul, mentioned above, called it a transformation that results in a renewal of the mind—a new way to think.[12] Those who get Christianity right have a *sustainable* culture that thrives through the enormous changes of twenty-one centuries! It is why there are billions of Christians in varied cultures around the world. They share a cultural lens, a compass that can fit any human culture. For example, when Christians from Mexico meet with Christians from Korea, it feels like family. Why? Because they share the same spiritual lens. They share a similar faith culture.

Could this work for Republicans and Democrats? Majority and minority leaders? Educated and minimally educated people? African Americans and Chinese Americans? Absolutely. In fact, it does. Values, beliefs, attitudes, priorities, and worldviews form a common bond beyond other linguistic, stylistic, or geographical differences. That is significance!

I know this from personal experience. I have taken groups of American Christians to work with Christians in many areas around the world. When we meet Christians in other places, the experience is like family! Even former Middle Eastern Muslims who are now Christians in the U.S. share this common spiritual culture. They are like brothers and sisters among other lifelong Christians from different backgrounds. The Bible says, "There is neither Jew nor Greek, there is neither slave

> **What if the UN had the culture compass?**

nor free, there is neither male nor female; for you are all one in Christ Jesus."[13] What if the members of the United Nations had the culture compass, while retaining their own individual geographic and cultural traits? I wonder, does anyone at the United Nations ever ask everyone to list their values? Beliefs? Attitudes? Priorities? Worldviews? Wouldn't that be a great way to start each year? Would that enhance their objectives? Have you ever listed these elements of your culture? Do you share them with your children?

Intrinsic Motivation

Jesus focused on intrinsic motivation. A culture-focused movement doesn't motivate people

> **People with intrinsic motivation are motivated to make a difference.**

with the "carrot and the stick." People with intrinsic motivation aren't driven by reward or punishment. Those with this cultural lens are motivated to make a difference. Civility inspires beyond success. Division demotivates. For example, if I wasn't motivated by intrinsic motivation, I would never go out to prune our trees. I'll never see them harvested. Nor would I write books. For me, it's too much work if the only payoff is royalties. You can make money as a priority, or you can make a difference first. Money, fame, and all the rest can be way down the list. You can be genuinely fulfilled. Making a difference is the fuel to make a difference.

Once, in Nigeria, I spoke to a crowd of 250,000 people (estimated by the Lagos newspaper the following day). Sometimes, in my travels, we set up a workshop at a hotel and two people attend. For me, my passion, drive, and energy are the same, regardless of the crowd size. Why?

My culture has grown. It's not about me. It's not about success. It's all about significance. Each person is important. The difference in fulfillment, attitude, and health is huge. Is your investment limited to this world and its future?

Intrinsic motivation provides a willingness to sacrifice and produce beyond the paycheck. Most pastors I've met would do

It is not the paycheck. It is character.

what they do for free, though they are grateful for remuneration to feed their families. I've met billionaires who share the same attitude. Intrinsically motivated people are energized by joy more than reward. The best Marines, the greatest sons and daughters, the hardest-working students, and the most productive workers all have this in common: It is not about the paycheck. It is not the brand name. It is not the title. It is not the promise of promotion. It is character. Character is a by-product of culture. You will jump through incredible hoops to accomplish what others consider impossible. You become a building block of a civilization that has a positive future. Anyone can flirt with success. World changers focus on significance.

Jesus led the way. The Bible says that Jesus, "...for the *joy* that was set before Him, endured the cross...."[14] If you catch the culture, if cultural elements are your compass, you become an amazing, intrinsically motivated person. You must decide. Is it a job or a calling? You can become a different person, a better person. You can do this. It begins with humility, the subject of our next chapter, and Lesson #3.

Chapter Five

Hard to Be Humble: Lesson #3

"If I cannot do great things, I can do small things in a great way."

— Napoleon Hill[1]

The world says arrogance is influential power. The world is wrong. Your influence to impact for good is much stronger from the position of genuine humility.

Can a member of Congress learn from a colleague of the other party? Can parents learn from their children? Can a police chief get wisdom from a beat cop? Can a CEO receive advice from the janitor? Can a pastor take input from that little old lady who's been at the church seventy years? Can you learn from others?

Of course you *can*. Do you have the will? If so, it is likely you have the power of humility, the bedrock of genuine

> **The power of humility is the bedrock of civility.**

respect. Jim Collins, in his book *Good to Great*, summarized a "great leader": "Profound humility and ferocious resolve."[2] If you are genuinely humble, you are teachable. If you can learn, you can grow, invent, re-create, and conquer complexities. If you can learn, you can experience legacy greatness.

Genuine humility requires confidence. It's an inside job, not a façade, program, or technique. Confidence—faith in God's plan—fosters the capacity to learn and grow. Also, you have the capacity to be wrong. With humility, it's not about *me*. It's about *us*. It's not the ego, but the goal. The solution is ultimately important. Breaking gridlock requires humility. Truly humble people are those who restore civility.

Life is a team activity. It's never just about you. So, you never conclude that you are always right...or that you have all the answers. "Team" implies you always make your best progress with others. It implies your commitment is to get along. In team sports, real superstars are not the athletes that are full of themselves. They are talented *team* players. The difference? Confidence plus humility.

Do you believe this myth? If you demonstrate humility, you are vulnerable, and you will lose your confidence. Steven Furtick says, "But, healthy confidence is born out of genuine humility.... Confidence without humility is arrogance. Humility without confidence is weakness."[3]

The word confidence comes from two Latin words: *con* and *fidem*, translated "with faith." Jesus, who walked the earth more than 2,000 years ago, described Himself as the "Son of God." It sounds arrogant at the extreme. Yet, His life is admired by believers and skeptics alike. He developed the most influential movement in history. Yet He is known for His humility!

We heard from Paul earlier. He is one of Jesus' well-known followers. He was changed from arrogance to humility after Jesus appeared to him on the road to Damascus. Later, Paul wrote this to the believers in Corinth:

> We sometimes tend to think we know all we need to know...but sometimes our humble hearts can help us more than our proud minds. We never really know

enough until we recognize that God alone knows it all.[4]

Paul's comments follow the wisdom of the Jewish proverb: "If you think you know it all, you're a fool for sure; real survivors learn wisdom from others."[5]

Gridlock

> **Gridlock is a form of human failure.**

When rebellious young adults land in prison, there is often a gridlock experience in their past: between them and their parents, teachers, the police, or society. When workers strike, there is usually an impasse between their company and rank-and-file workers. When urban citizens demonstrate, their frustration with police or city government has reached a stalemate. When political hearings drag on and on, the government stalls. Presidential executive orders are often the result. Let's call it for what it is: Gridlock is a form of human failure. Pride translates into stubbornness. Where is humility? What kind of behavior is that?

When gridlock occurs, there is always a lack of humility. People draw the line, take a stand, and quit communicating *with* one another. They start talking *at* each other. It occurs in families and in marriages. When it does, they lose their grip on civility. It ends in heartache. People withdraw—give up. Society is in deep trouble, marriages are fractured, people sue each other, and respect is in the toilet. That unique gift that makes us human disappears. Much of the news media subconsciously teaches us that this is "normal." Society suffers from mass depression.

78

Life suffers. Many are discouraged.

The Forgiving Side of Humility

Have you ever watched a congressional hearing where they grill someone about their alleged bad behavior thirty years before? Do you know anyone whose parents constantly remind their adult children of their wayward lives when they were in high school? Do you know anyone who, in a weakened and troubled season of life, did something that hurt their friend—and that friend unfriended them, not just electronically, but personally, forever?

Forgiveness is much more than an act. It is a perspective on life. In fact, Jesus said,

> Don't pick on people, jump on their failures, criticize their faults—unless, of course, you want the same treatment. That critical spirit has a way of boomeranging. It's easy to see a smudge on your neighbor's face and be oblivious to the ugly sneer on your own.[6]

Forgiveness is not simply an action. It is a worldview. It is looking into the mirror and honestly assessing your own imperfection. That assessment, reflecting humility, injects into your heart something this world desperately needs. It is called grace.

Perhaps you have heard the acronym for grace: "GRACE – God's Riches at Christ's Expense." Grace is undeserved kindness for people who are honest with who they see in the mirror. You are the greatest fool if you think you are perfect and, therefore, have the right to judge someone else who is not. If you are certain of your perfection, and right to judge, ask your spouse, parents, boss, or neighbor to weigh in on the subject. It will help you on the road to humility.

So, how should we respond to an impropriety that offends us? On this, Jesus has a great procedure. Step one: Go to the person *privately* and show the person where they are wrong or have wronged you. What, not on the six o'clock news?

> **Humility is something this world needs.**

No monologue by a late-night talk show host? No headlines in the newspaper? Right: one on one, privately. It's called human respect. But what if he continues the offense?

Step two: Take another person, a witness, and talk with the offender privately. This is called human kindness. Your conversation is not vengeful or arrogant. The goal is not embarrassment or to prove a point. It isn't an approach of arrogant superiority. In fact, the Scripture says, "...speak the truth in love."[7] This approach is a reflection of mature people of faith.

If the person acknowledges the offense and apologizes, it remains a private conversation. You have helped another person. You have not embarrassed them or kept a list of their wrongs with a "threat to go public," an act of cruel manipulation.

Step three: If the person refuses to change and continues their acknowledged offense, then it goes to a group of faithful, mature believers. The purpose, as always, is to protect a fellow human being and seek restoration.

Put yourself in the position of the offender. How would you like to be treated if you misbehaved badly? Would you want someone to approach you privately from the perspective of care and concern, to help you? Or would you like someone to leak it to the press? Or would you like them to gossip behind your back? Or would you want them to put it in an email, sent to all your friends, which is libel?

Many years ago, I trained a pastor to be a church consultant. My hope was that he would become part of our team. Instead, he took much of our "intellectual property," some tools and measurements we had developed over years of research. He used our materials, thinly disguised, in competition. I could have reported him to the authorities, which would have been easiest...but not best.

I confronted him one on one. It was not easy for me, and it wasn't comfortable for him. But there were no harsh words or attacks on his character. I simply pointed out that it was wrong, and I was disappointed. I made no threat and did nothing to embarrass him publicly.

A few years later, we met at a gathering of consultants, at the invitation of a denomination. I treated him with civility and as a friend. Later that day, he invited me to dinner and apologized. I forgave him, and we remain friends.

Honestly, this approach is not easy. But, in all humility, I'm not perfect. I've got my own weaknesses. I'm also open to correction. Why? I want to be my best self. In my weakness, I know God forgives me for my mistakes. In the prayer Jesus taught His followers, it says "...forgive us our sins (missteps/debts/infractions—whatever you call it) as we have forgiven those who sin against us."[8]

Do you see the connection between humility and forgiveness?

Forgiveness heals people. It is an act of love. It is a civil dimension unique to humanity. In our world today, don't you think we can do a lot better, treat each other with more kindness, and live with timeless values that restore one another?

It's Not Your Father's World

Technology has increased the rate of change. What worked yesterday doesn't always work today. In fact, some of what we did ten years ago is now irrelevant. The amount of change is increasing. The speed of change is accelerating. There are some who are wondering, "Can we survive what we are creating? Can we manage the speed of life?" We can, if we rediscover our moral compass. *Values never change, unless we lose them.*

> **Values never change, unless we lose them.**

In our rapidly "advancing" world, we all need to become adaptive. The landscape is changing in so many areas, how can you learn to navigate off the map? You can look at this as an impossible challenge...or an exciting adventure. It's your call! Have you considered the role of humility in all these changes?

As an adventure, living off the map is risky and sometimes lonely. Think about it: It seems more challenging than ever before to live at such a rapid pace. My colleague tells me I'm out of date because I don't have the latest, new phone. "It still works fine," is my reply—which impresses no one. I get it. We're on a new map. Yet, I don't get it. That's the challenge! To relearn, to grow, it takes humility.

It's tough, the pace of change. It takes a reorientation to a world that is a rapidly moving target—moving more quickly than ever before.

You can no longer live by inspiration alone. You must also live with exploration. You have to be a student and a learner. You can't do it if you are a know-it-all. It can only happen if you're humble and teachable. With all the change, you can learn a little about many things.

Yet, to excel, you need to learn a lot about a few things. That requires a team approach—which is a good idea, even in a marriage. Don't connect with just any team. Make sure it's a team of insatiable learners. Not for a season, but as a lifestyle. You can't do this without genuine humility. In his book *The Purpose Driven Life*, Rick Warren wrote, "Humility is not thinking less of yourself; it is thinking of yourself less."[9] You need to look at life as fluid, not static. Think of your family, business, school, government, or church—not as an institution, but as a living organism. Life is a moving target. You must reorient from maintenance to mission. You will move from rules to open options— where all the best ideas are welcome. You will change your worldview about life: from fixed pragmatic to an adventure. Your attitude will change from "we get it right" to "we can learn." Your posture will change from "we are proud" to "we are humble." Your self-image will reorient from "I'm in charge" to "I'm here to empower others."

Genuine humility allows you to grasp the distinctions between methods and principles. You need to be clear about methods. However, in a changing world, your methods can and will change. If they don't, you face disaster. When my grandparents went to school, they needed a pen or pencil and a pad of paper. When my grandchildren go to school, they have iPads or laptops. It is almost impossible to fathom what my great-grandchildren will use at school. Methods change!

Yet, this is the key: *Principles do not change.* My grandparents respected their teachers. My grandchildren will do the same, or they will not make it through school. They will not make it through life. My grandparents had to exercise discipline to finish well. My grandchildren will have to do the same. These are principles of life. They do not change.

Sadly, the evidence is clear. Some people have confused the flexibility of methods with the inflexibility of principles. They are stuck in methods that are now unproductive. Others have watered down the principles. A huge price is paid when principles fade.

In 1980, Alvin Toffler predicted, "The illiterate of the 21st century will not be those who cannot read or write, but those who cannot learn, unlearn, and relearn."[10] It's not simply about different answers. It's about framing different questions to diagnose the present—and future—realities. Above all, this requires genuine humility. If you're not humble, why would you learn, let alone relearn?

The founding fathers of the United States worked hard at developing "a more perfect union."[11] The value of this approach is not only what they wrote. It's what they didn't include. The structural details were not included. They likely realized that too many specifics would bog down the American government and paralyze the dynamic to adapt. Their approach is framed in humility. They knew some things. They had learned in the "old" country what didn't work. However, they didn't know it all. They were humble in spirit—often giving the greater credit to God. They were brilliant and humble. Many think that's contradictory. It isn't. It's essential!

However, over time, the natural tendency is for human beings to add additional laws, bylaws, and bureaucracies. This trend occurs in countries, Christian denominations, universities, even in families. It's a form of arrogance: lock in the future by relying on a law, a rule, for everything. Even the Jewish nation of the Old Testament wandered in this direction. The result? Gridlock. The *cause* is loss of humility...and trust.

As the world changes ever more rapidly, those who have a character of humility will be loyal to the principles and ruthlessly against mixing methods with cement. This is why, with regard to Washington, D.C., you sometimes hear leaders speak out against "big government."

> **Those who have humility will be loyal to the principles and ruthlessly against mixing methods with cement.**

Surely, you recognize our world today is greatly different than the world of even twenty years ago. The massive changes require that you constantly look for different methods that deliver the best results. If you are effective, you will keep the principles that serve as the backbone of life. This approach requires a profile of humility.

Methods and Principles

Methods are about deliverables, but principles revitalize life. In secularized America, we are now into the second and third generations of spiritual decline. Many churches are plateaued or declining. This is, sadly, a common cycle for a spiritual movement. This cycle has been repeated across the centuries, in many areas of the world. If you visit the great cathedrals of Europe, you see a remnant of vibrant faith, reflected today by monumental facilities reduced to museums and tourist attractions.

This spiritual cycle is coming around in England, where a few hundred churches, led by adaptive leaders, have changed the methods and resurrected the principles. We have visited these leaders each year for the last twenty years. We take church leaders from North America with us. They learn from these leaders about their commitment to biblical principles and their pragmatic commitment to flexible methods. That's what our visitors learn. What they *catch* is amazing humility and graciousness. How refreshing!

A U.S. politician of significant influence once reflected, "Intoxicated with unbroken success, we have become too self-sufficient to feel the necessity of redeeming and preserving grace; too proud to pray to the God that made us."[12] Who was that government leader known for his humility and faith? Abraham Lincoln!

Lincoln's comments came at a low point in the U.S. spiritual cycle. The pattern is the same elsewhere in world history. What happens? The principles allow a nation to flourish. In time, people move from worshipping the Creator to worshipping the creation—the blessings a principled nation receives. Humility shifts to arrogance. A nation drifts!

The cycle continues with increased corruption and disrespect for authority, laws, one another, and life itself. Chaos becomes the norm. There are seeds of destruction, similar to the fall of Rome. It doesn't mean everyone has abandoned God or the principles of the founding fathers. There are always some who remain faithful. However, lawlessness, corruption, greed, and misconduct increase.

Mahatma Gandhi said,

The seven deadly sins are:
Politics without principles.
Wealth without work.
Pleasure without conscience.
Knowledge without character.
Commerce without morality.
Worship without sacrifice.
Science without humanity.[13]

Sound familiar?

When speaking to different groups around the U.S., I ask people to compare a newscast today with one five years ago. The response is the same everywhere. People reflect discouragement. The percentage of people who are greatly troubled increases. Suicides have hit a higher level than at any time in recent history. Now, more people die each year by their own hand than in car accidents. Of course, automobiles are safer. Why do suicides continue to rise? Chaos produces hopelessness. Yet, hopelessness gives birth to humility.

Some wonder if their children will be killed by some maniac while they are in school. They wonder about those who are living illegally in our country, unsure if they will misbehave and harm their communities and families. Others feel their grandchildren will never collect Social Security because it will be bankrupt. Many fear drugs will take the lives of their offspring. They are uncertain whether their grandchildren will have solid, lasting marriages. The list goes on. Civilization deteriorates. Civility becomes rare. The humility process continues to build. God gets our attention.

Today, there are many signs of an unhealthy nation, troubled people, and an unprincipled society. Yet, there are signs emerging, indicating that more people recognize society cannot go on this way. All these challenges drain pride but increase humility. Fear leads to openness. At this point in the cycle, *the hunger for civility is powerful.* This is the climate in which people are hungry for hope.

Many are considering a new compass: a leap of faith in God. Others are returning to the faith of their former life—searching for the compass they put in the drawer years

> **More people recognize a society cannot go on this way.**

ago. Meanwhile, there is a slow but steady trend of churches adapting fresh methods to get eternal principles across to twenty-first century people. Those churches are growing and multiplying other churches, as they raise up respectful citizens. These churches are led by those who are humble. They are teachable. They are learners.

Churchgoing Christians are not perfect, nor do they perceive themselves as such. If they thought they were perfect, they would have no need for church—no need for God. There are, of course, horrendous evil activities committed by so-called Christians who have lost the principles of their faith. It proves God was right all along: People aren't perfect. There are also Christians and whole groups of churches that don't get it right. They throw out the principles. However, they are the exceptions rather than the norm. At the end of the day, God chose to rely on imperfect people!

Recently, I was consulting a church in Wisconsin. As part of my work, I toured their Christian school. Painted on the wall was another quote from Abraham Lincoln, "My concern is not whether God is on our side; my greatest concern is to be on God's side, for God is always right."[14] God is not only right, He is also loving and forgiving. It takes humility to accept His restoration.

Living in Humility

> The future belongs to those humble enough to be learners.

The future belongs to those humble enough to be learners, not self-declared experts. They will be open-minded. But they won't be so radically open-minded their brains fall out! In truth, *real* experts never stop learning. Are you one of them? If you're full of yourself, there's no room for God…or for others…or anything new.

Humility may be more important than intelligence. Humility allows for the emotional capacity to grow. New methods for this changing world cannot be imagined until your principles are clear. Humility is the window for discovering new possibilities. On

> Humility may be more important than intelligence.

the other hand, if you're "full of yourself," you have no room for new methods.

The renewal of a nation is not about discovering new data, programs, or techniques. It is about people, just like you, with the capacity to journey off the map into the future, into uncharted territory, with a good compass. This is how real breakthroughs are explored and applied. It is how civility is restored. You can't respect others if you're crowded out by yourself.

One of the greatest barriers to breakthrough is binary thinking. This is the trap waiting for you if you see solutions as either/or. You will

> **You can't respect others if you're crowded out by yourself.**

look at challenges and consider solutions that are either this or that. Genuine humility unleashes the energy to try and fail. To experiment without this or that. You will consider solutions that are totally and creatively new. They fuel the imagination beyond either/or to consider both/and. Both/and solutions develop teams, create unity, release power, and restore civility. With a firm hand on the compass—the principles, you have the freedom to explore barriers that would otherwise handcuff your ability to survive and thrive in a changing environment. How often do you see evidence of that in the news?

It seems odd, but it is true: Humility provides the stamina to explore new territory, where there are few absolutes and many questions. Humility is the climate in which you have the freedom to experiment and fail, to innovate without penalty.

As a parent, consider the environment of your home for your children. As a teacher, think what this

> **Humility: the freedom to innovate without penalty.**

would provide for students in your classroom. As a company leader, what would this do for workers? It's the environment that says, "You are free to improve your world, in an attempt to make this a better place to live and thrive." Consider a government that is not gridlocked by party spirit, rules, regulations, and customs. Leaders would be free to experiment and to inspire the future by innovating the present. Humility among government leaders diminishes prejudice. It clears the air to make progress for the constituents who put them there.

What about you? Do you have the humility to empower others to innovate? Can you accept the freedom to navigate the new territory of tomorrow? Are you prepared to join the adventure of learning that frees you to explore new methods that are more effective? Can you use what's best, even if it wasn't your idea? Probably not, unless you are truly humble.

Father Strickland, a Jesuit priest, said, "A man may do an immense deal of good, if he does not care who gets the credit for it."[15] An expression of Jesus' humility was His willingness to develop followers. This is the art of multiplying others to take over.

Jesus gathered twelve guys and poured His life into them for three years. At first blush, this seems like a ridiculous approach, given that His stated goal was to reach everyone on earth! He didn't call them members of His gang. He didn't even call them church members. He called them "disciples," which should be understood as "apprentices."

These guys weren't leaders of religion. Some were fishermen. Another was a tax collector. Think about how popular that guy was! Most of these guys had little or no education, as far as we know. They weren't leaders of anything important. So, why them?

Maybe Jesus wanted to make it clear to billions of His followers through the ages that anyone can be equipped and empowered to take part in the greatest movement to ever hit the planet. My point? God can use humble people. Proud people? Not so much! It takes humility to multiply yourself. It takes humility to consider multiplication more important than your own personal achievement.

Actually, it's humility plus trust. Jesus died and rose from the grave, and then He left town! Actually, He left the earth. In reality, He

> **God can use humble people. Proud people? Not so much!**

left the movement in the hands of a group of nobodies who had only three years of training. That's humility plus trust! Yet He said, "For where two or three are gathered in my name, there am I in the midst of them."[16] That takes humble faith to believe. Rick Warren said, in the *The Purpose Driven Life*, "The closer you get to Jesus, the less you need to promote yourself."[17] Rick caught the culture of Jesus.

If your goal is only and simply to become "successful," your vision is too small. Think of yourself less, and multiply.

> **If your goal is to become "successful," your vision is too small.**

For Jesus, the vision was to develop an approach that would ignite a movement. It has lasted twenty-one centuries. Jesus' movement has grown throughout the centuries. It is spreading like wildfire in many places today—in Africa, South America, India, China, and in thousands of churches led by people who get it.

> **Check your humility, get out your compass, and multiply yourself.**

So if you want to make a positive mark on this world, check your humility, get out your compass, and multiply yourself. Invest in others. This is the ultimate mark of humility: It's not all about you.

Humility means it's about others. No matter who you are, you can learn to live your own movement. It can occur with your kids, at your work, in your school, in government, or anywhere. You can learn this and do this if—and only if—you have genuine humility. If it's all about you, the road ends there. It ends with you. If you have true humility, the horizon is limitless. It is counterintuitive. If you are humble, you are teachable. You are a learner. You are a multiplier. It sounds unusual, but it's true: Our world desperately needs genuinely humble people. In the next chapter, we will add to humility the concept of organic living, which is Lesson #4.

Chapter Six

Organic Living: Lesson #4

"You change a country not merely by bolstering its laws but by transforming the hearts of the people."

— David Kinnaman[1]

The word "organic" refers to the *basic* makeup of something: an organization, a country, a group, or a person. "Organic" means "inherent," "inborn." It also means "constitutional." "Organic" is related to "organism," defined as a system of "various parts functioning together as a whole to maintain life." A marriage is an organism. So is a family. So is a nation. A productive organism has healthy organs—parts of the larger whole.

Your impact for civility grows as you do. With an organic worldview, you are always learning, always becoming. This lifestyle draws respect that grows on others. Live organically!

One of my all-time favorite books from graduate school was the classic written by George W. Peters, *A Biblical Theology of Missions.* Peters raises an interesting perception about how Jesus' approach focused on the vitality of people rather than building organizations. The implication? When people are healthy, the greater organization thrives. This is an organic approach. Peters writes:

> **When people are healthy, the greater organization thrives.**

Christ is the wisest of all philosophers. He is the wisdom of God, yet he founded no philosophical school. Christ is the greatest of all scholars and educators, yet he instituted no educational system. Christ is the greatest benefactor and philanthropist, yet he founded no social welfare society, institutions, or philanthropic foundations. Christ....[had the]...deepest concerns for freedom, social uplift, equality, moral reformation, and economic justice. Yet Christ founded no organizations or institutions to initiate, propagate, or implement.... [His] fundamental task was to build a bridge between God and man....[2]

Think about this: Jesus models a fascinating approach. It seems counterintuitive to our natural inclinations. We focus on building organizations—political parties, institutions, even religious denominations. Jesus focuses on the organic building block: each individual person. His focus is on you and me.

We can learn a lot from this organic approach Jesus used. His movement has produced more positive change in the world than perhaps any other. Are you tempted to disagree? If so, it's likely you are looking at human followers of Jesus who have sometimes messed up His approach, as in the Crusades. It's scary, but left in the hands of people, we don't always get Jesus' movement right. Yet, He uses people like us anyway. Perhaps He has more faith in us than we sometimes have in Him!

Jesus taught organically. He told numerous stories that reflect His cultural values. His stories described truths about a personal growth plan. He described the attitude of the farmer: patient, waiting for the harvest. He clarified priorities—watering the plants and watching for weeds that crowd out the crop. These metaphors are more than a guide for agribusiness. They are a cultural guide for every person—one person at a time. They are invaluable lessons for your life. They are the seeds for a civil society. God's plan is organic: It's all about planting, growing, and harvesting—using ordinary followers to achieve extraordinary, eternal results.

Organic Living

Your organic, spiritual life begins by *preparing the soil*. The soil is the medium where growth occurs. It is the climate. If you are wise, you will monitor your climate. What do you watch on TV? What do you read? Who do you listen to? Just like a gardener in Minnesota would have the wisdom to delay planting a garden in January, you should monitor your climate carefully. Timing is important! Make sure you protect yourself. Monitor the people who surround you. Are they critical, judgmental, or disrespectful? Do they represent a pessimistic darkness? Not much grows in the dark. Don't be fooled—your primary social group does have significant influence on you.

Farmers know the importance of fertilizer, lime, and all that determines the pH of the medium—the soil. They also know how important it is to remove weeds that rob the nutrients from the final product. Parents influence their children—well or poorly, or somewhere in between. Organic parents provide "fertilizing events."

For example, my parents struggled financially, but they sacrificed to make sure I was exposed to off-Broadway stage productions. At first, watching people sing and dance seemed cheesy, especially compared to playing football or shooting squirrels. However, it wasn't long before I fell in love with amazing productions like *Oklahoma!* and *The Phantom of the Opera*. They also took me to church. They got me a tutor when I struggled with high school algebra. My parents were enculturating me. They sacrificed to provide cultural fertilizer. They were cultural architects. I never got a lecture about their values and beliefs or about their attitudes toward love, family, God, country, or civil obedience. They didn't force-feed me with their priorities or worldviews. They simply and clearly lived their culture. They organically reflected the soil of their culture, even through the regular hugs they gave me—and my friends and girlfriends I brought home. They told every new friend, "just call me Mom," and "just call me Dad." (That freaked out my girlfriends at first.) Culture is more caught than taught. I caught it, and I'm grateful.

When my wife and I were married, I inherited a group of in-laws. My wife has five sisters—all married. My brothers-in-law all called my wife's parents "Ralph" and "Jenny." In spite of the unspoken social pressure to call them by their names, I just couldn't do it. My organic culture, growing up, made it feel "unnatural"—even disrespectful. So I took the risk and called them "Mom and Dad." Organically grown culture is powerful.

When a tree farmer prunes young trees, the objective is to remove competing limbs, resulting in a straight, high quality tree. The pruner cuts off one of the competing "Y" limbs at the top to straighten

> **The path to civility is developing people in a culture environment.**

the tree's growth. By removing the obstacle, the sun will actually pull the remaining top limb straight. That top limb is called a "leader." The work of developing a healthy stand of trees is called silvi*culture*. The path to civility is leading people in a culture, an environment. It is what Jesus did with His followers. It's an organic process that shapes lives. Have you ever been "pruned" by someone who wants to invest in you? Cultural architects lovingly prune. They know: Effective pruning works better with light than heat.

Good parents, with a compass, guide their children toward civility. If children don't respect their parents, why would they respect the laws? If people in

> **Cultural architects know: Effective pruning works better with light than heat.**

a nation are saturated with Hollywood films that glorify disrespect for law and order, how does that improve the society? If the political leadership reflects disrespect for each other, what does that teach the next generation? If opinionated talk show hosts disrespect our leaders, what is their organic influence on those watching?

Invitation and Challenge

Jesus provides an organic approach for the development of respectful followers: *invitation and challenge*. His invitation was simple. When He met a potential follower, He simply said, "Come follow me." You can't legislate civility. Jesus began with an invitation, "Would you like to come along with me? If so, I'll help develop you. I'll cultivate you to reach your potential—beyond your imagination." There was no political maneuvering. You don't create civility by majority vote. However, you can invite people into an organic environment, where they *catch* the culture. It's a growth process, with a lot of nurturing and pruning along the way. It is an organic approach.

Do you ever wonder about the systemic approach of disruptive elections in Congress? It often occurs when a new member of Congress is elected. Seasoned members frequently take that person "under their wing" and "show them the ropes." However, that is not the organic model! Jesus spent three years, 24/7. He prepared an inner circle of twelve young men. They launched the first phase of the greatest movement in history.

What if retired members of Congress returned to their home states, gathered a few young candidates, and organically nurtured them? You know, like...discipled them. What if part of the process was to prepare young, new leaders as future candidates to Congress? What if future politicians were mentored into political leadership? What if they focused on well-articulated culture: values and beliefs—the organic building blocks of civility? What if young candidates caught a posture, a culture of service? What if they learned respect as a fundamental principle? It could be a movement to take over Washington, D.C., with civility as the number one priority—and the party they represented would be a second priority to that culture.

Jesus' followers don't always follow His organic model. In my senior year of high school, I felt called to be a pastor. I talked to my minister, Pastor Vic, about how people become pastors. He said, "I'll take you to visit a Christian college. You go to that college for four years. After you graduate, you go to seminary for four more years." One of those seminary years is an intern year with a seasoned pastor.

After six years of theory, I was sent out to Florida for my "internship." I met my supervising pastor, who was a strong leader. Yet, he didn't organically mentor me during that year. He was busy leading his church and the denomination. I was considered a "helper" on his staff. The system in my denomination, like many, ignored organic mentoring development as Jesus modeled it. No wonder churches struggle! John F. Kennedy said, "Efforts and courage are not enough without purpose and direction."[3] The best guidance is provided by cultural architects. Jesus called it discipling. It is an organic growth approach.

After three years with Jesus, the twelve disciples moved from invitation to challenge. The challenge was no small objective: "Go into all the world and do what I did for you, make disciples, the same organic way. In this way, you develop followers of this movement."[4] Eleven of the twelve fell in love with the challenge. They lived it until they died. They multiplied themselves hundreds of times. The eleven were not "graduates," limited to knowledge. They were movement people. They were organically infected with respectful character. It wasn't simply what they did. It wasn't just head knowledge they learned. It was who they had become. The movement was not a "cult." Yet, the foundation was, undeniably, "culture."

> **The best guidance is provided by cultural architects.**

Many would agree that, for decades, the political part of our world has been somewhat stalled. Not many of those called "politicians" are practicing the central concept of being "polite." Very few demonstrate respect for those who disagree. Many work hard at getting enough votes to get their way. It seems that many don't focus much on listening or understanding the cultural elements of values, beliefs, attitudes, priorities, and worldviews of other politicians. They operate at a legislative level without much focus on the organic elements that form opinions.

It's not hard to find politicians forcing their opinions, debating on outcomes, arguing and symptom solving. Rarely, however, do you hear politicians asking—at an organic level: "Why do you hold that opinion? Can you explain it? What are your cultural values? What is your belief that drives your opinions? Why do you have that position? What is your priority in this discussion? Where are you coming from? What has been your real-world experience that drives your thought?" Rarely do you see politicians dedicated to the organic level of understanding one another. Sadly, most of their behavior is uncivilized. Where is the compass?

How Does Organic Development Work?

Organically preparing others in civil obedience is not difficult. There are six steps. (We reviewed them briefly in Chapter Three.) These steps, used by Jesus, work universally. This approach develops character by catching the culture from someone who has it. The process is simple, but profound. It is obvious, but rarely

> **The process builds character... transformed lives.**

practiced in political circles. Soldiers, physicians, plumbers, pilots, and others learn "on the job." More than head knowledge, organic training builds character. The result is not simply academically educated followers, but transformed lives. This is what our world desperately needs: respectful movement people. Anyone can follow these six organic growth steps.

Step One: "Want to hang out with me?" This is *invitation,* discussed previously. It is the opportunity to be equipped at a movement level. When a person begins development, it is important to catch the compass culture. This doesn't occur as an academic lesson. It is caught more than taught. When the cultural elements are caught, they become the framework of life. They are firmly embedded in your personal world. This is the slow process of enculturation.

Step Two: I do/you watch. Organic developers do not throw people out of the boat in order to teach them how to swim. Watching the leader in operation is invaluable. There is no quick fix to civility. It's like growing a crop. It takes time.

I love watching the quarterback passing drills at an NFL training camp. Both the starting quarterback and the second string quarterback throw to receivers, running the same routes at the same time. This is *precision mimicking.* It's amazing how their movements become identical. The starting quarterback is practicing. The second string quarterback is watching, learning, and practicing. The coach is watching. So is the receiver coach, to observe the routes. The receivers are not simply catching a football. They are catching what can't be taught. This is the best way to raise kids—or anyone, including politicians. But there is much more.

Step Three: I do/you help. This stage models *safe partnership.* As an organic developer of people, you invite the follower to "put a toe in the water." It's a baby step. However, the important part? You are right there, serving as a safety net if it does not go well. Your follower now enters the stage of "becoming." As my friend Peter Brierley says,

"You are what you have been becoming. Your past with all its heredity and development has helped to fashion you as you are now. But the question is not now 'Where are you?' or 'What are you doing here?' but 'What do you see...yourself becoming? What, where, who will you be in ten years' time?'"[5]

Step Four: You do/I help. This is the gentle organic step of *nurturing productivity.* It is the culture of a garden in the growth process. The "gardener" waters and weeds—in process. The "disciple" is ready for action, on a limited level. Meanwhile, you serve as a safety net.

In this step, you momentarily give the work to the one who is being developed. This is far beyond head knowledge. It is knowledge put to action. Yet, it is knowledge put to action without much risk. When does the NFL coach put the second string quarterback in the game even if the starter is healthy? Fourth quarter, five minutes to go, we've got the ball, and we're ahead by two touchdowns. No one you organically develop can or should move from "zero to a hundred" the first time out. Why? They are still catching the culture. Incremental growth is the organic approach.

Step Five: You do/I watch. In this step, you develop *potential independence* in your disciple. The disciple begins developing the cultural lifestyle to "go and do likewise." This is the *challenge* part of *invitation and challenge.* At this stage of organic development, you are demonstrating stability and avoiding dependence. President Harry S. Truman said, "You can accomplish anything in life, provided that you do not mind who gets the credit."[6]

To do this, you must be a confident, secure, and stable person. You find fulfillment in multiplication. Many parents have one or two children. Some have none. Few have six to ten, or more. However, if you are a parent of, for example, five children, if each marries and has five children, you can be a grandparent to twenty-five grandchildren. Most grandparents are thrilled when the grandchildren visit. It's one of those multiplication moments: "Look at what we started!" Grandparents are just as happy to see the grandchildren leave. Why? They have learned two lessons: (1) multiplication is marvelous, and (2) it would kill you to parent twenty-five children!

Step Six: This step is all about letting go. It is called *respected independence.* It begins the process of multiplication. The next generation has caught the culture. The compass that got *you* here will take *them* there. The challenge: "Go do it." Even if the methods change, the compass remains—the productive culture continues. Jesus does this. In the Bible, followers of Jesus are called the "children" of God. This represents the power of multiplication.

Parents: at step number six, you let go. You are stable and secure parents of a family of families. If you don't let go, you become insecure parents who meddle in the lives of your adult children. This frustrates adult children. As parents, you feel a sense of rejection, which you earned. Good parents let go. Poor parents control. The movement they birthed becomes an area of resentment.

For Jesus' followers, the challenge was huge: "Go make disciples of everyone in the world, anyone who will ever

Organic Development Six Steps

- Invitation
- Precision Mimicking
- Safe Partnership
- Nurturing Productivity
- Potential Independence
- Respected Independence

Result: Geometric cultural multiplication: a movement!

be born." Yeah, that's a big challenge. Honestly? Many Christians and churches aren't up to the task. Why? They don't multiply organically. They don't live the six simple steps. Sadly, many Christians have abandoned the approach modeled by Jesus and sold out to the quick fix!

> **The quick-fix focus is naïve. Organic multiplication is up close and personal.**

They do programs or beg for volunteers. Their focus is naïve: Preach and teach crowds. No one can disciple crowds. Organic multiplication is up close and personal, by definition. It takes time. It's like raising kids.

Organic Growth

If you are a good gardener, you don't dig up the plants to see if they are growing. If you are a good mentor, you equip others like good parents raise their children. And, as you "let go," you reemphasize multiplication culture: "Now, you do what I have done: Disciple others through the six organic steps. Meanwhile, I will do the same." This is not a program. It becomes a lifestyle. It represents a movement. It works in every dimension of life—if you work the organic plan. People catch the culture. This is the fine art of discipling, also called apprenticing. You don't just learn the job; you catch the culture.

> **If you work the organic plan, people catch the culture.**

In the Far East, people plant a tree called Chinese bamboo. During the first four years, they water and fertilize the plant with seemingly little or no results. Then, the fifth year, they again apply water and fertilizer—and in five weeks' time, the tree grows ninety feet in height! Did the Chinese bamboo tree grow ninety feet in five weeks, or did it grow ninety feet in five years? The answer is: It grew ninety feet in five years. Why? Because if, at any time during those five years, the people had stopped watering and fertilizing the tree, it would have died. How are you nurturing civility in others by what you say and by what you do?

Multiplication takes patience. On our tree farm, we replant little trees where one has died. Three or four years later, when we are pruning, it is not unusual to discover two trees six inches apart. What happened? We replanted a tree next to one that appeared dead. However, underground, the roots were alive. Growing people, like growing trees, takes time. Leaders too often give up on a person just when they are about to blossom. What is "above ground" is visible. What is "underneath," inside a person, is invisible. If you want to grow respect in others, your role is to protect the roots, nurture the "tree," and watch for what comes. It may arrive in a different season of life. Don't ever give up on anyone.

We live at a time when civility seems so absent, we are tempted to give up and quit trying. Instead, continue to water and fertilize others, nurturing the seeds you planted in them. Practice perseverance and endurance. Developing another person doesn't always bear fruit. But when it does, the joy and the power of multiplication are worth it. Multiplying yourself is awesome! Ask any parent with a newborn baby.

> **Building culture, instilling values, is long, hard work.**

In any group of people, there is the danger of drift from organic, bottom-up culture to a bureaucratic, top-down, control-oriented approach. Why? Because building culture, instilling values, is long, hard work. However, the bureaucratic approach dramatically changes the ideology and alters the basic DNA of the movement. The decentralized, adaptable, organic organism becomes a static, top-down organization. This tendency toward bureaucracy and top-down organization can occur in families, governments ("big government"), and churches (denominations).

A healthy movement is like a starfish. A top-down bureaucracy is like a spider. In their book *The Starfish and the Spider*, Ori Brafman and Rod Beckstrom contrast two types of organizations. In the bureaucracy, with top-down leadership, it's like a spider. If you cut off the head of a spider, it dies. A movement is like a starfish. If you cut off a piece of a starfish, it grows back. And the piece you cut off? It becomes another starfish.[7] The DNA multiplies.

The movement Jesus started was fueled by starfish-like cultural DNA. When groups of people, like nations, multiply over time, the DNA normally keeps the cultural distinctions. However, when a country grows in numbers of people and the DNA, the cultural values, are

> When a country grows and cultural values are de-emphasized, what made the country great now contributes to its decline.

de-emphasized—or lost, what made the country great, now absent, contributes to its decline. The country increasingly relies on laws, rules, and big government. The European Union is facing this challenge today. Rapid and massive immigration has occurred with little opportunity for immigrants to "catch" the culture of their new countries and enrich the country with the best of their own cultures. This causes culture shock for everyone.

The over-organized structure of big government results from an inability to change in a changing world. The bureaucracy is like placing the future in handcuffs. The compass, replaced by rules, becomes diminished. There is a tendency to elevate methods to a level that is sacred—untouchable. This is the beginning of irrelevance. What got you here won't likely take you there.

A nation becomes susceptible to drift in the area of principles. Why? Everyone is focused on methods. This cripples movement. Organic, bottom-up culture drifts into high-control fixation on methods! "We've always done it that way."

When it comes to raising respectful children, parents who fall from the organic approach become reactive and overbearing. They are now known as "helicopter parents." They hover over their children, especially as the children become teenagers. This top-down trend sows seeds of a coming rebellion. In institutions of learning, it turns the propagation of values into liberal influencers of propaganda. Professors teach students *what* to think rather than *how* to think. In this way, they abuse their position and purpose. The result? The organic culture is gone. Mark Twain once said, "I never let my schooling interfere with my education."[8]

If you live an organic life, you will focus on cultural growth that multiplies into a movement. Consider how important culture is to the process. Consider how you approach life through the lens of culture: values, beliefs, attitudes, priorities, and worldviews. Growing a garden is called horti*culture*. The process of growing trees, as mentioned before, is described as silvi*culture*. Vaccines are grown in a *culture*, in a petri dish. The greatest movement on the planet, Christianity, is developed around the culture of the Kingdom of God.

Consider many of the challenges we face today. Most of them are the result of cultural neglect. This is the failure of institutions to keep

> **The word culture...reflects "a strong commitment to principles."**

pace during a time of rapid advances. The word *culture* comes from the word *cult*, which has negative implications. However, the original meaning reflects the notion "to care for," "a strong commitment to principles."

Top-down regulations kill a movement—like removing oxygen from the atmosphere. Life by control destroys motivation, encouragement, and vision. It changes the focus from "doing the right things" to "doing things right." It is a change in focus: from principles to procedures. However, the organic life keeps you and others centered on core competencies, even when you face unhealthy challenges of drift in the environment.

Contextualization vs. Syncretism

To remain centered, two realities are important. These two realities are directly opposite dimensions. *Contextualization* is placing proven cultural elements into the present context. In order to build on what has proven best, *utilize "containers" and ideas that speak the language of the present context.* Contextualization is like focusing on the same values, but using modern words.

The challenge comes when leaders confuse contextualization with *syncretism. Syncretism is when you change values, beliefs, attitudes, priorities, and worldviews to become popular by "syncing up" with cultural drift.* Ignoring the non-negotiables of what got you here, you get the idea that you will gain influence by doing, believing, and acting like whatever others find popular—without a compass of values, beliefs, attitudes, priorities, and worldviews. It is sometimes called liberalism. This approach leads to the demise of whole cultures, entire civilizations. Why? It leads to cultural drift. It destroys the strong cultural elements that first allowed a culture to thrive.

Top-down pressure leads to rebellion. Children raised by heavy-handed parents rebel. Workers distanced from company leadership resort to paycheck motivation. This is the lowest form of motivation. It produces the poorest results. The work gets sloppy. The end product or service has less value in the marketplace. The company loses market share. The end is near.

Major League Baseball coaches who fail to connect with their players contribute to a losing team. Legislators who lose touch with constituents become massively irrelevant. When leaders of denominations push institutional agendas, they literally smother the power of God in local churches. Jesus said, "…upon this rock I will build my church;..."[9] That "rock" was the confession that Jesus is the Son of God, the Savior of the world. It validates all of His teachings.

It's impossible to stop a movement, except through dry rot from within. The greatest enemy of a nation isn't the hostile country with nukes. You

> It's impossible to stop a movement, except through dry rot from within.

can see those coming. It's the moral decay of principles that made it great in the first place. The Roman Empire had the power and might to rule the world. It disintegrated because it moved from a brilliant culture to a cesspool of moral decay. The empire never recovered.

An organic movement impacts the world. Lasting impact does not originate in institutions, buildings, programs, or creeds. Movements are alive. They grow. Organic influencers move movements. They are on offense rather than defense. They always have the ball. There are no defenders on the squad.[10]

Low Control/High Accountability

A healthy movement is the organic development of low control balanced by high accountability. How do you operate? You have four choices:

1. Low control/low accountability. This is a plan for chaos and revolution.

2. High control/high accountability. This is a plan to stifle creativity and adaptability. It produces low production and low ownership. It is the approach of a dictator.

3. High control/low accountability. This is the socialism or monarch model. It results in low productivity and raises the potential for anarchy through instability of the masses.

4. Low control/high accountability honors the initiative of everyone. This is the "democracy" model: The people hold the ruling power. Each person has responsibility, which requires accountability. As a "republic," the supreme power rests in all citizens, who are entitled

> **A healthy movement is low control balanced by high accountability.**

to vote. It is exercised by representatives elected by the people, who hold them to a high level of accountability. This approach is the formula for a movement. It stimulates production and fuels creativity.

John Edmund Kaiser, in his book *Winning on Purpose*, reflects on high control in the former Soviet Union. Kaiser reports:

> In the days of the Soviet Union, what was the difference between taking a road trip in Russia and a road trip in Nebraska? For either one you would have needed an automobile, fuel, and a driver. But in Russia, you would need one thing more that you would not need in Nebraska: permission. Travel in a totalitarian state is based on approval. Travel in a free country is based on authorization—as long as you operate the vehicle within a few simple traffic laws, you are free to drive wherever you need to go.

Kaiser focuses on bureaucracy in churches, but it relates to every organization:

> [Leading in a bureaucratic maze] is like taking a road trip in the Soviet Union: You are not surrounded by Communists, but it's hard to get the resources, it's hard to get permission, and it's hard not to feel that you're stuck in a previous century. And yet, the proper use of a few clear boundaries can create the freedom and authority leaders need to accomplish the mission.[11]

This raises the question about big government, more rules, more regulations. This is your choice: Will you recycle because you honor God's creation and have legacy thinking for the next generation? Or will you recycle when the law says you must do so or get penalized?

Do you really want more laws...and less freedom to do the right thing? If your children don't turn off the lights when they leave the room, they lack ownership. They don't pay the bills! As a cultural issue, parents have a choice: focus on rules (high control) with consequences, or develop a culture: the civility—respect—of saving your parents' money and being a good manager of world resources. This cultural lesson is not about lights or bills. It is a culture about the value of resources that has universal applications. It is about the cultural element of values. Do you really want more rules, more laws...and less freedom to do the right thing?

Ownership is developed in a collaborative culture. Organic input holds a culture together through personal ownership. Dwight D. Eisenhower said, "You do not lead by hitting people over the head— that's assault, not leadership."[12] When followers accept the culture of the leader, it becomes a way of life. When leaders fail to lead organically, it signals the decline of civilization.

You can get people to "follow the rules" through high control, but it is a temporary fix. It is more effective to nurture others toward living the culture. Does it take longer? Yes! Lee Iacocca, a former president of Ford Motor Company, commented on what has made America great. He said,

The greatness of America wasn't because the country was rich in natural resources: it was because people dug into the ground and took them out, often under terrible conditions. It wasn't because of miles of open prairies: it was because people broke their backs to till the soil. It wasn't because of a few industrial geniuses: it was because millions of people fired the furnaces and stamped the metal. And it wasn't because of a piece of paper called a Constitution: it was because people fought, and sometimes died to fulfill its promise of a just and humane society.[13]

Low control/high accountability changes a good family into a great family. It changes a good company into a great company. It changes a good school into a great school. It changes a good community into a great community. It changes a good nation into a great nation. In the next chapter, we look at Lesson #5: four ways to build respect.

Chapter Seven

Four Ways to Build Respect: Lesson #5

"No one really knows why they're alive until they know what they'd die for."

— Martin Luther King, Jr.[1]

Would you like to increase your influence of respect among others? Before Jesus developed culture, He

> **A loving, respectful, healthy culture does not exist without people.**

developed people. A loving, respectful, healthy culture does not exist without people, those just like you and me. People matter to Jesus. In his own words, He gave His life— He died—for people. In this chapter, we will discover four powerful ways you can flavor your world with decency, respect, and kindness.

*Respect is contagious. It's caught when you share a **vision** for a better future. It is consistent when you stick to your **values**. Respect is communicated by your **vocabulary**. Your delivery system for building respect includes **vehicles**—use them. You can make a positive difference!*

Listening to some talk show hosts, politicians, and news reporters, I can't believe the way they speak about others. The Apostle Paul wrote letters to new Christians in young churches during the first century. In one of those letters, he says, "Be gracious in your speech. The goal is to bring out the best in others in a conversation, not put them down, not cut them out."[2] He also wrote, "Therefore encourage one another and build one another up, just as you are doing."[3]

Do you live for people? Or do you live to make money? Or do you live for entertainment? Jesus didn't spend much time on this planet. What—maybe 33 years? He didn't go public until His last three years. During that time, He influenced a few, and they turned the world upside down. Or, perhaps more accurately, right-side up. Do you think our world needs improvement today?

By design, Jesus' followers gathered in relational communities called churches or congregations. They are supposed to be the best of what we call "community." It's easy to demonstrate that Jesus and His followers had a commitment to improve this world—one person at a time. Those, in what are called churches, were intended to spread love, forgiveness, respect, restoration, and decency. The primary role of a pastor or priest is to equip God's people for ministry, service to others. The objective? To make the world a better place by sharing God's love. Is every Christian, every church, perfect? No. But they have tasted divine love and forgiveness, and they should want that for everyone.

> **Faith in God is an act of respect.**

As challenged as they may appear, communities of Christian believers represent the most powerful, longest lasting, difference-making group in world history. Why? Part of the answer is the structure. They are supposed to operate like a family. The glue is love: for Jesus, for one another, and for others not yet in the family. It's not the profile many would choose to change the world. Few would have predicted their long-lasting history. Faith in God is an act of respect: for your Creator, for His creation, for other human beings. Respect and faith are unconditionally connected.

The glue? Dr. Henry Cloud says, "Your brain runs on three things—oxygen, glucose, and relationships."[4] The entire movement Jesus launched is built on relationships. Christians around the world share the same spiritual culture. Churches grow through relationships. The Christian's primary "mission field" consists of those with whom they have a relationship.

Whoever you are, wherever you live, whatever you do, your health, your vitality is built on respectful relationships. Why? The power of impact is *relational influence*. In a world of violence, gossip, hatred, and bigotry, those you trust are the people with whom you have a relationship. Relationships are everything!

Relationships of respect are the glue that holds a group together. Challenges become easier to bear. Through relational support, you can adapt to change. You can support one another. Even though change is uncomfortable, relationships provide a reservoir of resilience. If you want healthy relationships, you must build trust.

However, your trust is always on trial, under attack, subject to drift, and vulnerable to outside temptations.

> **If you want healthy relationships, you must build trust.**

Relationships without forgiveness are doomed to fail. Forgiveness is a by-product of love. Forgiveness is a non-negotiable element of civilization. Forgiveness is unique to humans. Hatred, unwillingness to forgive, disrespect—these are uncivilized elements.

Relational communities survive in spite of outside pressure. They can adapt to this changing world. However, changing a healthy culture is non-negotiable. Those who try self-destruct. When the culture is strong, the structure is flexible. When you develop a healthy culture, you have an environment that provides stability when everything else is changing.

As a parent, how much effort do you devote to building family culture? When you look at the person in the mirror, what emphasis do you give to the DNA of your values, beliefs, attitudes, priorities, and worldviews? How much do you invest in the culture of others? Your answer measures the level of respect you have for those in the human family.

A healthy, respectful culture gives the freedom to change, adapt, improve, and innovate. It is the constant island in the rough seas of

> **Respectful culture gives the freedom to change...and innovate.**

change. Most Christians share a similar, biblical worldview. It can be described as "thinking like Jesus." It is being interested in the same things in which God has interest. It is called a biblical worldview. The Bible says, "Since Jesus went through everything you're going through, and more, learn to *think like him*. Think of your sufferings as a weaning from that old sinful habit of always expecting to get your own way. Then you'll be able to live out your days free to pursue what God wants instead of being tyrannized by what you want."[5] Would this concept improve the climate of disrespect in our world? I think it would. A consumer mentality is not all bad, unless it rules your life.

During different times of history, there have been occasions when a contentious spirit has gripped the U.S. Congress. It has occurred elsewhere, in other countries, as well. The citizens of the U.K. divided about the decision to exit the European Union. Israelis and Palestinians have deeply rooted opinions about Israel. Several Central American countries have struggled with the corruption of political leaders. The list can change from time to time, but there are always serious struggles somewhere on planet Earth.

Most often, those struggles bring out disrespectful behavior among human beings. Do you wonder if focusing on cultural issues could help define those tensions? How often do you hear basic issues focused on values, beliefs, attitudes, priorities, and worldviews? How much are these cultural elements the real issues behind the challenges?

Could it be that governments have not practiced enough culture building? When people are not on the same page, a clearly articulated culture can bring everyone together in thinking, through respectful conversations and, ultimately, votes. But when most citizens become entrenched, gridlock occurs. It is a scenario of "divide and conquer." Could it be that relationship building has become a lower priority? Is there a need for intentional culture building? Wouldn't it be great if everyone would explain *why* they stand on certain positions? Would that increase communication? Provide clarity? Would that improve civility?

Four Building Systems Modeled by Jesus

Culture leaks. No matter where you look, no matter who you are, culture simply fades by attrition. When a nation is divided, in the middle of a culture war, culture requires more focus. When your family grows, cultural stability requires more attention. This is where culture-building systems are valuable.

> **No matter who you are, culture simply fades by attrition.**

There are four prominent culture builders. I call them the four V's:

1. Vision
2. Values
3. Vocabulary
4. Vehicles

It is surprising how often people fail to recognize and utilize these four building blocks of culture. As you are bombarded daily by diverse opinions and disrespectful behavior, use the four V's to consistently maintain and build civil culture. Why? Because culture is always subject to drift.

1. Vision

Vision is your best hope and dream for a preferable future. It includes details about how you get there. It is clear enough to explain to anyone— in a way they can remember. Unlike "wishful thinking," a vision is a doable strategy.

The Bible says, "Where there is no vision, the people perish."[6] In another translation, that verse says, "Where there is no revelation, people cast off restraint;..."[7] It seems like a complicated statement, yet it is very helpful. "When there is no revelation" applies to those who have no guidance from God. In a secularized nation, there are many people who are biblically unaware. Their culture has had no input from faith. They have had no biblical base. This is not a judgment.

Actually, Christians are complicit. Many believers fail to share their faith. Churches have ineffective strategies to reach those who do not know the culture of Christ. Our conflicted culture is partially a result of the failure of the Christian movement. So, many people have no "revelation." They "don't listen to God," who speaks from His Word—the Bible.

For this to make sense, you need to look at the other half of the sentence: "people cast off restraint;…" What does that mean? It signifies that many have given up their right to say "no" to anything, including bad ideas. In Scripture, it means, "If you don't listen to God, you give up your right to say 'no' to anything. It implies that you say 'yes' to everything."

Think about this vision concept in a family. If children don't listen to God or their parents, they give up their power to say "no"—to drugs, violence, sex, unhealthy habits, poor choices of friends—the list goes on. All this because of no vision, lack of vision, or a corrupted vision. If you have no use for God, basically you disrespect your Creator. It's a small step from there to

> **If you have no use for God, basically you disrespect your Creator.**

disrespect your parents, your own health and safety, the law, and relationships.

Consider this issue in the political arena. If you have a division among politicians at a level where they won't listen or meet with one another and work things out, they are giving up their right to vote. It's called gridlock. They are not doing the job for which people "hired" them (voted for them)! Even if they do communicate with one another, on what level do they communicate? Do they drill down to the five cultural dimensions? Or, are they symptom solving and talking past each other? That raises the question, are they really leaders? Or are they managers? They are supposed to be leaders. Are they leading with ignorance? Or with bias? This leads to responses that are reactionary, rather than actionary. It raises the question, "With our civilization at stake, are they doing their job?" Gridlock leads to disrespect from constituents.

The news media frequently get sound bites from leaders. Do they ask, "What is the issue behind the issue?" What is the person's position based on values? Beliefs? Attitudes? Priorities? Worldviews? The big question? "Why?" On what grounds have you taken this stand? Most often, those of us receiving media "news" don't get past the background noise! This is related to vision-building.

Oswald Chambers says this about vision:

Vision involves optimism and hope. The pessimist sees difficulty in every opportunity. The optimist sees opportunity in every difficulty. The pessimist tends to hold back people of vision from pushing ahead. Caution has its role to play. We all live in a real world of limitation and inertia. Cautious Christians draw valuable lessons from history and tradition, but are in danger of being chained to the past. The person who sees the difficulty so clearly that he does not discern the possibilities cannot inspire a vision in others.[8]

Do you know people who see difficulty in every opportunity? What happens after a while? You don't even want to be around them! It becomes an avoidance reaction. My wife had a relative like that. At family gatherings, whenever I saw him coming, I tried to avoid him. I'm embarrassed to admit it, but he would wear me out. No matter what the subject, he could make anybody feel depressed or frustrated in ten minutes. If he caught you, he would talk incessantly. Do you know why? He couldn't find anyone else who would listen to him. I have a friend whose parents are like that. How sad!

If you choose to be a champion for civility, become a vision caster. Vision is related to clear purpose. Do the people around you hear you cast vision? If I interviewed your friends, would I hear about your vision? Do those who work with you know your vision

> **Do you have a vision for your country?**

clearly? Do you know the vision of the politicians who got your vote? Do you cast vision for your children? Do you have a vision for your country? Can you articulate it?

Vision is used as a servant, not as a master. It is a container for values and beliefs. Vision is a vehicle that reflects your attitude. It is the expression of your worldview. Vision sets your priorities. It is a future scenario. Vision builds respect. How? People admire those with a clear vision.

There is a severe challenge in the area of vision: Individuals cast vision; groups do not. The climate of a group tends to swing toward the status quo. That's why those who cast vision get the reputation of being "visionaries." Here's the challenge: Congress is run by a lot of committees. Corporations have boards of directors; schools have boards; churches have councils, boards, deacons, or elders. Hospitals have boards. Boards—groups of people—don't cast vision. Controlling groups eat vision for lunch. They swallow visionaries. They often don't attract visionaries. They lean to the side of control. Think about life today. How much does our world need visionaries?

Helen Keller lost her sight at nineteen months old. Yet, she is famous for this comment: "Worse than being blind is to have sight but no vision."[9] Visionaries see what others can't. They see farther than others do. Think of the thousands of people in hundreds of countries who act like their country should have elected them! Have you heard this comment? "It's interesting that the only people who seem to know how to run this country drive cabs or cut hair." There is a difference between vision and opinions. Opinionated noise generators are everywhere! Are you an opinionator or a visionary?

> **Opinionated noise generators are everywhere!**

In a downward-spiraling, unhealthy culture, some are opinionated from the platform of ignorance. Sometimes it sounds like so many are smarter than their leaders, there could be thousands of presidents, senators, governors, police chiefs, family doctors, and pastors! But none of them are remotely qualified, beyond their own opinions. Basically, they disrespect their leaders. Casting vision is an *earned* right and responsibility. If you want the license to cast vision for others, you must earn the leader's job! If you get the leader's job, you'd better cast vision!

Vision casting is an important element of building respect, refreshing culture, and reframing ideas. One thing is certain—vision leaks. The insidious lack of respect proves it. In truth, most people do not cast vision often enough. It may be because they are

> **Visionaries ignite passion by casting vision.**

not visionaries! Visionaries ignite passion by casting vision. My friend Joe says, "It's not what the vision is, but what the vision does. Vision moves people to action." It has been said, "Poor eyes limit how far you can see. Poor vision limits how far you can go."[10] When you *earn* respect, you receive respect. Visionary leaders ignite passion. Passion produces more than a paycheck. Those who catch a vision catch fire. They no longer have a job. They have a calling! They are on a mission. Vision is related to the compass. It points to the direction.

2. Values

Values reflect those issues that are most important. Values define what you live for. Values determine what you would die for. Values are what you consider to be precious. Values drive your behavior. Values earn and develop respect. As the saying goes, "If you don't stand for anything, you'll fall for everything."

As mentioned in an earlier chapter, values are important for developing a culture. However, values are more than attributes of culture. Physicist Albert Einstein said, "Try not to be a person of success. Rather, be someone of value."[11] Most cultural architects have values as part of their culture. Are you valuable to others? Do others see you as a *person of value?*

> **Do others see you as a person of value?**

There are two dimensions of values. (1) You have values. (2) You are a value to others. You *are* valuable because you *add* value to others. Do you make others better? If so, it means that you add value to them. When you add value, you earn respect.

As the owner of a tree removal company, I treated my workers very well. I "outworked" them on every job. Then, as a pastor, if I got a call at 3 a.m. from a church family in a domestic impasse, or a spouse who reported the death of her husband, I was there. Those efforts earned respect. It empowered my leadership. I used that respect to challenge our people to reach out, cross-culturally, to our community. The result? The respect I earned was translated into higher respect for God's mission and for those in our community.

When I realized God was calling me to serve Him full time, that decision was strongly influenced by the desire to add value—to add *eternal* value to others. If a teacher doesn't have a passion to add value to his students, should he teach? If you are a parent, will your children say, at your funeral, that you added value to their lives? Adding value builds respect.

It's a challenge to add value. Being nice and respectful to those you momentarily meet gives you the opportunity to add value. When I'm at a restaurant and place my order, I ask for the name of my waiter. That tells him I consider him to be of value, a valuable person. I want him to know I don't *use* people. Everyone has value. When the waiter brings the food, I ask him, by name, "Dennis, I'm going to pray over this food. Is there anything I can pray for you, anything at all?" I know many waiters and waitresses are not practicing Christians. But you would be surprised how they respond and say how thankful they are.

It is not hard to treat another as a person of value. It shows respect. If you race through an intersection as the yellow light turns red, it shows disrespect. It also shows you have little or no respect for others—or their lives. When you cut in line at the amusement park, it shows you value yourself more than others. You disrespect others. They value you a lot less, too!

If you travel often, you spend time in hotels. When you get on the elevator and someone is in it, do you say, "Good morning?" When you pass a person from housekeeping in the hall, do you say, "Thank you for your service?" At an airport, you must go through security. This is an inconvenient reality of our declining civilization. Those who work in security are there to protect you, but you may dislike the feeling that you're being treated like a criminal—if just for a few minutes. Security workers are not the enemy. Yet, they take a lot of grief. Did you ever consider saying, "Thank you for keeping us safe"? I started doing this, and almost always, they say, "Thanks. We appreciate that." It adds a sense of value to their work and to them. Guess what? It adds value to my attitude, as well! Adding value earns respect and grows self-respect simultaneously.

When a society loses its core values, it is on a dangerous path. When people don't view others as people of value, civilization implodes. When media personalities or talk show hosts make fun of leaders, it's disrespectful.

> **When a society loses its core values, it is on a dangerous path.**

When educators are prohibited by law from expressing values to students, policemen are needed to patrol schools. When parents fail to clarify values, children end up in prison. When Wall Street ignores values, greed results in market collapse. When a manufacturer fails to instill values among workers, shoddy work leads to company bankruptcy. When Congress misplaces the compass of values, it results in leadership meltdown. There are reasons why studies show politicians rank lowest in respectful influence. If you don't add value, perhaps you should be replaced. Ask yourself, "How could I become more valuable to others?"

3. Vocabulary

Words are one of the most common containers that carry meaning. In the Bible, Jesus is called the Word of God who became flesh. Vocabulary transports ideas, thoughts, dreams, frustrations, love, hate, hope, despair. The use of words is a significant responsibility. Are your words always respectful—full of respect?

Words develop meaning. Meaning defines purpose. Purpose delivers direction. Direction drives impact. Wow!

Words are powerful!

Words are powerful! Do you treat them with the respect their power warrants? French philosopher and mathematician Blaise Pascal said, "Kind words do not cost much. Though they do not cost much, they accomplish much. They make other people good-natured."[12]

Remember that culture is *caught* more than taught. Children catch vocabulary from the culture of their parents, friends, television, books, movies, and the Internet. The vocabulary and the meaning it carries become the norm for the next generation. Vocabulary influences behavior. You use vocabulary that either encourages or discourages respect for others. My friend Walt Kallestad says, "You may know the proverb that states that it takes a thousand positive words to overcome one negative word."[13] The culture in which a child becomes an adult impacts the future of a nation. Words help shape that culture.

Preachers who use old, worn-out, irrelevant words to describe a living faith unintentionally bury the faith in the cemetery of history. Worn-out language from centuries past makes churches museums of irrelevance. Business leaders influence workers with words of hope or despair, and the company reaps the consequences. Politicians use vocabulary that unites or divides. They encourage or discourage public confidence.

When the news media speaks with conscious or subconscious bias, they provide more heat than light. The agenda shifts from reporting facts to providing opinions. If they present challenges from a cesspool of unprofessional journalism, it divides husbands and wives, parents and children. Public words encourage or depress a nation. Does your choice of words generate respect or disrespect? Do you own that responsibility?

Social media may be technology the human race has the knowledge to create, but lacks the moral maturity to use. Citizen journalism rips into issues, charged with more emotion than content. It reflects the immoral, disrespectful assumption that you can publish information without doing the homework to check your sources. It launches a backlash among increasing numbers of people who bail from "news," increasing the danger of an uninformed nation. Do you, like millions, unfriend others because of their disrespectful vocabulary? Do you bail from media that has become muddy?

Words are powerful vehicles: for good or for bad. Do you remember what they used to ask you in court? "Do you swear to

> **When God is gone, truth is optional.**

tell the truth, the whole truth, and nothing but the truth, so help you God?" When God is gone, truth is optional. Welcome to a fake world. This represents the power of words, for good...or for destruction.

Vocabulary is subconsciously lodged in your brain, your personal, private dictionary. Many films use vulgar language, considered unacceptable a few years ago. However, words are more than a sum total of their letters. They represent images in your brain.

Vocabulary like the "f-bomb" shows up in films and television. Words creep into your mind, then into your mouth, across your lips, and then into society. The imagery behind the words carries subtle pictures.

Actually, films would be just as good without the crude vocabulary. So, what is the point? What is the purpose? What is the cultural influence—even on you—inside, subconsciously? How does that help the national culture? How does that contribute to the best of civilization? To the next generation of our children?

Words can enlighten. I'm not a police officer, and there are none in my family. However, I have been horrified by the number of deaths of police officers. I am without *words* to think of the instances when a person walks up to an officer who is eating lunch in a restaurant and kills him. But I can recruit words that heal.

I decided, anytime I see an officer—at the mall, at an airport, at a concert or a restaurant—I'm going to walk up and say, "Thank you for your service." I've added, "Be safe." They don't know it, but that's a prayer. Most often, I hear words back, "I appreciate that!" This is an act of respect: for officers, for their service, for life. While it is not my intention, I even earn respect—I get respect back. Do you see how easy it would be to launch a movement of respect—and begin to change the culture of a nation? That is the power of vocabulary!

You can launch a vocabulary movement. It doesn't seem like much, but it's a war for civility. Building a culture of kindness, respect, appreciation, and decency has to start somewhere. When will it start with you? You can argue with words, but you can also heal.

> **You can argue with words, but you can also heal.**

Words have power!

4. Vehicles

There are thousands of vehicles on the road to civility! Not one of them is a car or truck. *You* are a vehicle. Jesus said to His followers, "Let me tell you why you are here. You are here to be salt-seasoning that brings out the God-flavors on this earth. If you lose your saltiness, how will people taste godliness? You've lost your usefulness and will end up in the garbage."[14]

Everyone communicates. Everything we see carries a message. The cleanliness of the restrooms at the restaurant reflects the value of what comes from the kitchen. The dress code of a teenage guy or girl can signal sexual abstinence or an invitation. The professional conduct of a receptionist sends a signal about the quality of the company's product. It is cultural clarification by vehicles.

When the person in the car ahead of you on the freeway throws out a hamburger wrapper, she is polluting her world...and yours! The cleanliness of your home may impact the future of pollution in the atmosphere—by your kids. Posting the great sayings of world leaders in the hallways of your elementary school is like investing gold in future leaders. The hours put in by the CEO impact the work ethic of those in the shop. The car that flies by you as you obey the speed limit forecasts something about the value of life. The incredible rise in suicides says something about the health and vitality of civilization. They are all vehicles.

The size and number of television screens in your home could signal the challenges your son might face concerning study habits at college. The truck with a loud muffler and the two Confederate flags in the back communicates the work that is yet to be done about human diversity and acceptance. The film subjects, language, and violence from Hollywood indicate a reason to be nervous about the future of the nation's direction. The declining attendance at churches and the rising median age of attendees signals more about ignorance of effective outreach than the lack of receptivity to a vibrant faith.

The increased abuse of alcohol reflects the emotional pain and stress of a nation. The epidemic of opioids reflects a troubled population. The slight decrease in teen pregnancies may reflect a change in morals, the use of birth control, or both. The stock market reflects the work-related optimism or pessimism the public has for the economic future. The frequency of viral videos demonstrates how the world is connected. The troubled spots around the world communicate the fragile level of peace. These are all vehicles, and they carry significant influence.

When you communicate, you choose a vehicle. Your choice carries your communication. It also

> **How you communicate is a moral and social responsibility.**

communicates itself. How you use that vehicle is a moral and social responsibility. You can demonstrate respect or undermine it.

Gossip has always been a vicious weapon in the hands of "loose cannons." A gossip is a person who says negative things about one person to a third party. It's the coward's approach to conflict. Gossip is a vehicle that greatly undermines the value of respect. With the power of social media, gossip is a demon on steroids. The remedy is covered in Jesus' teachings. He says, "If someone offends you, go to the person alone and share your perception of their fault."[15] If that were practiced, even by most Christians, the world of pain would be significantly smaller. Jesus' approach is all about respect.

Social media is a vehicle. You can send an email and use it for good, noble, and respectful communication. Or, you can use email to lash out against someone who has hurt you, and copy it to all your friends. Then, it becomes an evil epidemic already in progress.

Your car is a vehicle. It can take you places or it can kill you and others. Your car can carry groceries to the homeless or provide a place to have illicit sex in the back seat. Vehicles are powerful, for good or evil. The difference is in how you choose to use vehicles. Not just your car, but your phone, your house, your dress codes, your tattoos—everything.

The vehicle is the medium. The medium—the delivery system—is part of the message. I could tell you that someone gave you a million dollars. I could use English as the medium. I could call you. I could send you a letter. I could visit you personally. I could buy you coffee at Starbucks. I could send you a text. I could tell you in Chinese. They are all vehicles. Your audience and your message dictate your vehicle of choice. Choose wisely.

If you get a nasty email that unfairly criticizes you and it's copied to twenty people, what do you do? Most people would take their cue from the medium that sent it—email. And many would fire back their response copied to all the same people. It's your choice—to start an *un*civil war. The person who sent it was disrespectful. Your best response? Ask to meet one on one, privately, just the two of you.

If you want to be a champion for civility, you'll think long and hard about all the dimensions of the vehicles you choose—the delivery systems for your messages. When issues are sensitive, your choice of vehicle may be as important as the message. Not long ago, I asked this wonderful woman, Wendy, who works at our office, to pick up some small Christian cards I could use to say "thank you" or "I'm thinking of you." She got three packages, but one used old English words—which I would never use. I had a choice. I could just drop them off at the office and attach a note: "I don't use old English." But I wanted to make sure she knew I wasn't angry and that I really appreciated the other two packages. So I stopped by the office on the way to the airport. She heard my tone of voice and appreciation as I said, "It's no big deal. I didn't open them; just take them back—no rush." And I gave her a hug of appreciation.

Hugs are vehicles, too. In the early church, the local congregation was like an extended family. There was a lot of persecution going on at that time, much of it focused against Christians. This was especially true for the believers in Rome. In fact, they suffered persecution, even to death. Their pastor, Paul, wrote to them, "Greet one another with a holy kiss."[16] In that culture, it likely meant more than a business handshake. It was a kiss on both cheeks. In many Eastern cultures, that practice continues today. In Western culture, I believe that vehicle would be a "holy" hug. As an Anglo, I recently visited an all-black church called Impact in Detroit. Everyone I met hugged me—everyone. The only white guy of 200 in worship! It's the friendliest church I have ever visited! Based on the amount of pain and stress in our culture, I wonder if this hug vehicle should be practiced more.

I realize that suggesting we hug more at church is a sensitive subject. Why? The #MeToo movement is a reaction to incivility

> **Hugs are vehicles, too.**

KENT R. HUNTER

practiced by those in powerful positions who have abused women. It reflects physical disrespect. The #MeToo movement underscores the importance of civility at a very personal level. How do human beings interact? Is touch off the table? What is acceptable? A pat on the back? Or a handshake? What about a "high five?" Is it just about men and women, or does it apply to those of the same gender, as well? See how uncivil behavior diminishes even how we greet one another? Those who abuse women abuse the whole culture!

Do you see how disrespectful behavior puts everyone on edge? Human beings are complex communicators. We interact with more than words. Good communication includes the use of our eyes, body language, tone of voice, and touch. What about all the hurting people who say they need a hand on the shoulder, a handshake with two hands—and a squeeze, or a hug?

How do we get back to holy respect without losing the power of touch? First, we realize that human beings are part of a complex creation. Some need touch for assurance, encouragement, and support. Others do not. Second, Jesus taught how we should respond if we are uncomfortable or offended. This was mentioned earlier, but should be unpacked again at this point. The reference is from Jesus' teaching in Matthew 18:15-17. Jesus taught that if you are offended, in any way, you should tell the person right away. If you are the offender, you should apologize and respect the person's unique definition of their space and touch.

What if the offense is repeated by the same person? You confront the person again, with a witness present. If that doesn't work, you take it to the authorities. This means that you don't wait to confront the person years later or when they become "successful" or choose to run for public office. To do so is disrespectful to your offender.

This is how civility works. Vehicles make an impact. In a culture of disruption and tension, so many need to know they are loved in a *wholesome* way. For many, a hug is a vehicle of personal respect. For others, it's an invasion of privacy. Do you see the value of sensitive civility?

My point? As a cultural architect, recognize that you have many choices of vehicles to carry your message. So, stop, consider your choices, and pick the one that represents your best contribution to a more civil society. Vehicles deliver meaning. They influence content. Choose them respectfully!

In the next chapter, we will look at Lesson #6: the amazing power of story. Story is a special, unique, and powerful vehicle for cultivating cultural respect.

Chapter Eight
The Power of Story: Lesson #6

"Story is atomic. It is perpetual energy and can power a city. Story is the one thing that can hold a human being's attention for hours. Nobody can look away from a good story."

— Donald Miller[1]

Your story is important. You have stories that reflect respect. With all the bad news, you can provide personal stories of good news—and change the toxic atmosphere. Others will respect you—and catch respect.

What do Romeo and Juliet, the Star Wars franchise, and the Gospel of John have in common? They are great stories! The Bible is loaded with awesome stories. Stories shape culture. Ivan Illich was once asked, "What is the most revolutionary way to change society; is it violent revolution or is it gradual reform?" He gave a careful answer: "Neither. If you want to change society, then you must tell an alternative story."[2]

Stories shape people who shape culture.

Stories shape people who shape culture: in government, in families, in corporations, in universities, in nations, and in churches...one person at a time.

Do you like good stories? When I was a young boy, my parents took me to see the movie *The Greatest Story Ever Told*, based on the novel by Fulton Oursler. It is the story of Jesus. It planted a seed of curiosity in my mind. Years later, it blossomed to active faith that completely changed my life and directed my career path. That story, through me, has impacted the lives of hundreds of thousands of people on six continents through our work with Christian leaders. Who would know? It was the *greatest* story ever told, to me, in many ways! There is great power in stories.

The life and work of Jesus *is* a great story. It is actually a story of stories. Jesus taught the culture of faith, primarily through stories. How do you communicate your view of culture? Do you share a culture of respect? One of your best tools is the power of story. Ed Catmull, CEO of Pixar, says, "Stories communicate at a deep level. Stories are the way we communicate with each other. Stories are going to change the world."[3]

> **When you share stories...you build civility.**

As I was writing this chapter, I was headed home from a book signing at a Barnes and Noble in Phoenix. I was there to autograph copies of my most recent book. I had so much fun—and it wasn't just because people were interested in the book. I'm glad they were, but I met so many interesting people. In so many words, I asked several people to share their stories. I met some real characters! Everyone had stories. Sure, I believe my book will benefit them. But I really had fun with them, hearing their stories! These "customers" left as friends. When you share stories, do you know what you do? You build civility. When you actively listen to someone's stories, do you know what you do? You demonstrate respect.

Stories have a great way of influencing people and their cultural DNA. Consider how stories impact values, shape beliefs, develop attitudes, challenge priorities, and open up new, expanded worldviews. John Kotter says, "Over the years I have become convinced that we learn best—and change—from hearing stories that strike a chord with us...."[4] I couldn't agree more! Are you a storyteller? Or do you keep your stories to yourself? Everyone has stories. Share them. They make life interesting!

We have frequent guests at our home. As we engage in conversation, I often slip into a story. It might be about our tree farm, a church I consulted, or an event at one of my teaching conferences in the Amazon jungle, Japan, or somewhere else. I include details to paint pictures. My stories are not just to entertain, but to add value. Since my wife has heard these stories—several times—she sometimes interrupts: "Can you get to the point?" I think that my wife, as a preschool teacher, should know about the power of story. However, her mind is elsewhere: "Dinner's getting cold!" I'm the storyteller. She's the pragmatist. It's a good balance. And, I just told you part of our story!

Much of the narrative of Jesus' life is revealed in the four "gospels" of the New Testament in the Bible. The word "gospel" is a writing that focuses on "good news" about God. Most of Jesus' teachings are stories revealing truth about *life with God*. Another way to describe it would be *spiritual culture*. Jesus' stories, sometimes called "parables," describe how Christian culture is unique, helpful, or different from what you usually see in the world.

Stories that Influence

If you want to become an influencer using stories, Jesus provides a great model. His stories are simple. It was Ralph Waldo Emerson who said,

"To be simple is to be great."[5] Though Jesus' stories are simple enough for a child, they are deep enough to challenge adults. That's what you want to achieve with your stories.

Jesus' stories, and the entire Bible, have been a source for growing respectful culture throughout history. At a challenging moment in history, President Woodrow Wilson said, "There are a good many problems before the American people today, and before me as president. But I expect to find the solution to those problems just in the proportion that I am faithful to the study of the Word of God."[6]

Pope John Paul II wrote, "America first proclaimed its independence on the basis of self-evident moral truths. America will remain a beacon of freedom for the world as it stands by those moral truths which are the very heart of its historical experience…and so America: if you want peace, work for justice. If you want justice, defend life. If you want life, embrace truth—truth revealed by God."[7]

Stories can be humorous, but carry a powerful message, like this one reported in the Minneapolis Star-Tribune:

Three-year-old Katie was taken to her pediatrician during a recent bout with the flu. As the doctor examined her ears, he asked, "Will I find Big Bird in here?"

Apprehensively, Katie replied, "No."

Then, before examining her throat, the doctor asked, "Will I find the Cookie Monster in here?"

Again, "No."

Finally, listening to her heart, the doctor asked, "Will

I find Barney in here?"

With conviction, Katie looked him directly in the eye and said, "No, Jesus is in my heart. Barney is on my underwear."[8]

No matter who you are, your stories are powerful. If you have lived more than fifteen years, you already have hundreds of stories about your life. Most of them have a

> **Stories are your greatest gift to build respectful culture.**

valuable lesson you can share with others. As you go through life, from this day forward, when something happens in your life, think of it as a story you can use to invest a life lesson in another person. Stories are your greatest gift to build respectful culture.

Most people are hungry for good, positive stories. Contributions from Hollywood are mixed. Some are positive for building culture. Others are negative. Some that are negative teach what not to do. Violent video games are reported as a contributor to deadly massacres orchestrated by young adults. Watch what you watch! Stories are powerful—good or bad! The popularity of television series about government reflects the best and the worst of our culture. The same is true of "police" shows.

If you think about it, most leaders in history have used stories to cast vision, set agendas, raise hope, and describe challenges. Those stories are agents of influence, an extension of their cultural priorities. As you read them, notice how they draw mental images and promote important cultural issues:

John F. Kennedy: "But Goethe tells us in his greatest poem that Faust lost the liberty of his soul when he said to the passing moment: 'Stay, thou art so fair.' And our liberty, too, is endangered if we pause for the passing moment, if we rest on our achievements, if we resist the pace of progress. For time and the world do not stand still. Change is the law of life. And those who look only to the past or the present are certain to miss the future."[9]

Abraham Lincoln: "I desire so to conduct the affairs of this administration that if at the end, when I come to lay down the reins of power, I have lost every other friend on earth, I shall at least have one friend left, and that friend shall be down inside of me."[10]

Winston Churchill: "I would say to the House as I said to those who have joined this Government, I have nothing to offer but blood, toil, tears, and sweat. We have before us an ordeal of the most grievous kind. We have before us many long months of toil and struggle. You ask what is our policy? I will say, it is to wage war with all our might, with all the strength that God can give us, to wage war against a monstrous tyranny never surpassed in the dark, lamentable catalog of human crime. You ask what is our aim? I can answer in one word: Victory. Victory at all cost. Victory in spite of all terror. Victory however long and hard the road may be. For without victory there is no survival."[11]

Nelson Mandela: "Difficulties break some men but make others. No ax is sharp enough to cut the soul of a sinner who keeps on trying, one armed with the hope that he will rise even in the end.

"A fundamental concern for others in our individual and community lives would go a long way in making the world the better place we so passionately dream of.

"For to be free is not merely to cast off one's chains, but to live in a way that respects and enhances the freedom of others."[12]

Jesus, the Storyteller

There is a great narrative in the Bible about stories and what they can accomplish. It comes after Jesus had told a number of stories to build a new spiritual culture in His disciples. The disciples wondered why Jesus used so many stories. His answer is a powerful gift of understanding. Here is the backstory: Jesus had been teaching a group of people in a house. This house was near the Sea of Galilee. After teaching, Jesus went out and sat on the beach. Almost immediately a crowd gathered along the shoreline. It was crowded, so Jesus got into a boat. He went a little distance from the shore and spoke to the crowd. The Bible says:

> He addressed the group, telling stories. Sometime afterward, the disciples, his closest followers, came up and asked Jesus, "Why do you tell stories?" He replied, "You've been given insight into God's kingdom. You know how it works. Not everybody has this gift, this insight; it hasn't been given to them. Whenever someone has a ready heart for this, the insights and understandings flow freely. But if there is no readiness, any trace of *receptivity* soon disappears. *That's why I tell stories: to create*

143

readiness, to nudge the people toward receptive insight. In their present state they can stare till doom's day and not see it, listen till they're blue in the face and not get it.[13]

After Jesus rose from the dead, He appeared to many people over several days, including a large crowd. He said to the crowd, "By the power of the Holy Spirit, you will be witnesses of Me all over the world."[14] "Witnessing," for many people, brings back unpleasant memories of religious zealots knocking on doors, interrupting dinner. However, in the sense that the Bible uses the term "witnessing," it is very different.

> **Relationship glue multiplies the power for stories.**

"Witnessing" is like a witness in a courtroom trial. It isn't shoving the Bible down some stranger's throat. A true witness is someone who can say, "I was there. I saw it. It happened to me." Jesus told the crowds about anyone who chooses to follow Him. He said, "Be a witness." He was simply saying: "Tell your 'God stories.'" Christians do occasionally share their God stories with strangers if the issue comes up. But the most productive strategy is to witness to those with whom you already have a relationship, when they show receptivity. *Relationship glue multiplies the power for stories.*

So, what is your takeaway as a cultural architect? (1) Develop relationships with those in your social network. (2) "Disciple" others: Grow them in that relationship to multiply yourself so that they can tell their stories. (3) Continue expanding the reach of *strategic relationships* and powerful stories. (4) Never miss an opportunity to encourage civility: respect for others. That formula will grow your relationships and the culture. It will impact anyone you influence at the level of multiplication. Every human being should work to make the world a better place. Anyone can invest in others. You can become a

Cultural Architect
- Develop relationships
- Grow disciples
- Expand relationships
- Encourage civility

"movement" for good. Simply tell your positive stories. How much do you think our world needs that?

When I was in sixth grade, I already had a history of being a poor student. I didn't like school, and I don't think the school liked me. My attitude? "Why do we have to learn all this stuff?" Then, in seventh grade, there was this younger guy teaching geography. He started the first day of class telling his personal story. I thought, "This is the first teacher I've met who is actually a human being!" Then he wanted to hear our stories. In retrospect, my educational journey turned around that year. It was that teacher. It was his use of stories.

This issue surfaces one of the most fascinating concepts about stories in recent history. Love it or hate it, the following reference is either about an adaptive leader or a new storytelling mechanism that will flop. (Time will tell, probably after we are dead.) As mentioned before, President Donald Trump chose Twitter to speak directly to millions of constituents.[15] Those who, for whatever reason, choose not to be on his Twitter feed receive the information anyway. The media outlets and news programs multiply them, in praise or criticism!

Social Media

There's no question: President Trump's Twitter account is a message machine, loved by some and hated by others. *It is a huge and immediate platform for stories.* It's used mostly for factual reports, opinions, judgments, and debate. When he provides narratives of his positive experiences, he utilizes the most valuable power of stories.

What about the important element of relationships? Does the "Twitter machine" fail because most of those who get the tweet will never have a relationship with a president? Or, if you are that visible in the media, does a "media relationship" count? Or, is a president (or anyone, for that matter) with the Twitter feed *building* relationships?

This grand experiment may be one of the most fascinating attempts at using the power of stories. Consider this: Even though many of the president's Twitter messages are not stories, the news outlets add narrative, and they *become* stories. Interesting! If it demonstrates success, every leader should rethink the power of story influence by way of electronic distribution. If it flops, it will self-destruct, and it won't require an "act of Congress." Either way, the power of influence depends greatly on the type of stories told through electronic media.

What about you? How do you use social media? What if tens of thousands of people put their positive stories of respectful acts of civility on social media? Could you counter the bad habits of disrespect with a flood of positive, civil acts, multiplied electronically? There are many ways to influence civility!

> **Shape stories that help, not hurt; build, not destroy; and create, not wreck.**

We all have the responsibility to shape stories that help, not hurt; build, not destroy; and create, not wreck. What electronic stories do you share with your children, fellow workers, students, or constituent voters? Twitter may go away. The power of stories will not.

What about the children in your life? Another grand experiment is the influence of Pixar on future generations. With the power of technology, stories have evolved for children. From *Mister Roger's Neighborhood* to *Sesame Street* to amazing cinematography, the power of story is coaching a new generation of future leaders. How are you telling your story through the media available to you? Further, how are you designing your message to provide cultural DNA for the next generation to run this world? How are you promoting respect? Watch carefully what the kids watch!

Communicating Pictures

There are important reasons that libraries (both physical and virtual) are filled with literature and theaters are packed for films and stage productions. They all represent good stories. Television and the Internet provide thousands of stories 24/7.

Stories entertain, yet they are not neutral. The word "entertain" has the root meaning "to maintain" or "hold together." The contemporary meaning is described "to keep the interest of and give pleasure, to direct; amuse." When you show hospitality to someone, you "entertain." However, when you allow yourself to think about an issue, you "entertain" the idea. When people introduce themselves to others, they often use stories.

When you tell stories to build culture, you are entertaining (engaging, influencing) on many levels. When you use humor, your effectiveness increases. Former President Barack Obama had a gift in telling humorous stories. Throughout his presidency, he was an outstanding communicator. His use of humor made him personable, even to those who never met him.

In my career, I speak to many groups every year. I am convinced that, if I integrate appropriate humor in the form of a story early on in a presentation, I "have the crowd." My commitment is not to entertain, but to engage the audience. The main goal, however, is to enhance culture, the serious stuff. My effort is enhanced by a humorous story. Yours will be as well.

This is where some preachers drive me nuts. They are so serious, they are boring. If preachers are happy about how much God loves them, they should show some joy. These religious types who are so serious so much of the time become a liability to the Christian movement! They act like they were baptized in vinegar. If they were among Jesus' original disciples, I'm sure they would have been voted off the island! What about you? Do you share the joy? Joyful people attract others. No one is looking for help to be further depressed.

When you carefully craft stories, you create pictures in the minds of others. When these pictures

> **Stories create pictures in the minds of others.**

reflect the future, your stories cast vision. Like everyone else, there will be times when you get busy, dealing with life as it happens. It will feel like you have little time, energy, or creativity to look to the future. Give yourself time to recapture your vision. Remember, if you have no vision for the future, you possess no power for the present! Take time to dream!

When they first opened Disney World in Orlando, Florida, Walt

Disney had already died. At the opening, someone commented, "Too bad Walt couldn't see this." One of Disney's leaders responded immediately, "Walt did see it. That's why it's here!"

Tell your future vision stories. They will energize people to get from here to there. Give your heart time to dream. Darrow Miller said, "The earth will be filled with what is in our hearts and minds. If our minds are empty, our world will be barren."[16]

In your storytelling, use visuals. Not long ago, I was invited to speak to a large group of leaders from all over the U.S. and several other countries. They were gathered at one of the Disney World hotels. The leader of the conference assigned my time slot. It was at the end of a long day, from 4 p.m. until 5:30 p.m. It was the last session. I was told that the previous speakers ran over, so there was no time for a break before or during my presentation. The hotel needed the ballroom for something else, so we had to finish promptly at 5:30 p.m. The odds seemed stacked against me!

A "brilliant" idea came to mind as I made my way to the podium. I'm sure it was from God...or indigestion, I'm not sure. The media guy put a mic on me with a long cord. As soon as the mic was on, I started speaking: "Wow! You have been here for a long day. You must be really committed, or ought to be...committed! I'm told we have no time for a bathroom break. Now, if you have to use the restroom, feel free. I'm not here to torture you, but to help you."

I continued, "You might wonder how I'm going to make it through. I certainly can't leave and go to the restroom during this session." At this point, I put the mic cord up so everyone could see it. "You might think I was just being mic'd up, but you are wrong. You see, I'm prepared. It's actually a catheter...." The crowd roared. I had them with an impromptu story I made up in thirty seconds!

It was a little risky, but the roaring laughter put everybody at ease. My point? The mic cord served as a visual. It helped me get my story across. Visual aids are everywhere! Connect visuals with stories. Your audience becomes more receptive to the important stuff.

Civility is a serious topic. The future of the nation may rest on whether we reclaim respect for our leaders, for God, for our nation, for its heritage. Yet, some humor will always engage people. It helps people let down their defenses. Humor adds a bright spot to the many concerns we should have about civil disobedience. However, don't confuse humor with the disrespectful monologues given by some late-night talk show hosts!

One of my favorite visuals about humor was on the inside of a toilet seat on a train from Sheffield to London, England. It isn't unusual to find a sign on a public toilet, especially on a train or an airplane, to tell you what you shouldn't be flushing down the toilet. But on this train, the company was creative. The message read, "Please don't flush nappies, sanitary towels, paper towels, gum, old telephones, unpaid bills, junk mail, your ex's sweater, hopes, dreams, or goldfish down the toilet."[17] (I hope no one was outside the bathroom door, listening to my laughter and wondering....) In our serious world, with all the criticism, a little laughter is like medicine for the soul.

If you use an amazing story with a little humor, you can turn a "tough" message into humor. Humor is great to add to stories that are difficult for people to hear. Suppose you have to announce something people find uncomfortable. When this occurs, work hard to preclude the challenge by integrating the Mary Poppins rule: "A spoonful of sugar helps the medicine go down."[18] Weave into your stories encouraging examples of success. Success stories also balance challenging news. You are respecting your audience's needs. Anyone can appreciate a little encouragement.

Tell stories to your children. Parents, tell stories to your children. Make sure the stories include the values you want your children to learn. Tell stories that underscore what you believe. Don't let anything interfere with the stories you tell your children. This is how you reflect your culture.

The excuse some parents use goes like this: "I'm going to let my children make up their own minds about values when they get older, so I don't mess up their freedom." I have news for you. The head start about how culture has worked for you is your greatest gift to them. Further, if (at the moment) they're not buying it, the fact that you shared it won't make any difference once they get older. There is no danger of interference. Children grow up and make their own choices.

Don't handicap your children by refusing to share your values, the culture that works for you. Share age-appropriate stories that relate and provide a framework for making intelligent choices. Stories are your friend. They help you pass on the best of your culture to the next generation. Remember, culture is "caught" more than taught.

Interrogative Influence

Interrogative influence is a powerful tool to use with stories. It is the dynamic of asking questions. Some questions seek information.

Questions can disarm hostile responses.

151

Other questions serve to narrow the discussion. Often, questions turn issues from "heat to light" by removing stress in the conversation. Questions can disarm hostile responses.

Sometimes, even when you know the answer, your best approach is to ask a question. It frames the person's thinking. By using a question, you lay the groundwork for what you want them to hear…and adopt. You begin with a dialogue, not a lecture. A question is a vital asset to stories about culture. Questions guide movements. Engagement, through questions, is a pleasant way to build civility.

Someone asked St. Augustine, "What was God doing before He created the universe?" Augustine responded, "He was busy creating hell for people who are too curious about such matters!"[19] That is a humorous short story. But it could relax a person before you share your story about faith and eternity.

Jesus used interrogative influence with His disciples. It is the fine art of asking good questions. He provides a great example of how it works. After the disciples had been with Jesus for some time, He asked them, "Who do people say the Son of Man is?" The disciples had heard a lot of gossip around the marketplace. They had several answers, none of which were correct. Of course, Jesus had heard it all. In fact, His big question wasn't that question anyway. He was getting them in the right frame of mind for the real question. It is an excellent approach used by great leaders.

Jesus got to the point with the disciples: "And how about you? Who do you say I am?" Peter answered, "You're the Christ…the Son of the living God."[20] Jesus discovered what He wanted to know: (1) they get it; (2) they were ready for His departure. Interrogative influence is the concept of asking questions instead of telling people what you want them to hear. The benefit? They are engaged. The result? You have greater impact. Smart!

It seems like many in our world today are critical or judgmental. Some appear as self-appointed experts. They speak on subjects about which they know just enough to be dangerous. Opinion polls are popular reports about "serious issues," yet they are treated like a beauty contest. This is not the greatest failure. The real challenge is the increasing inability to identify the right questions. When you tell stories, be sure to ask the right questions. Asking the right question frames the discussion.

> **Asking the right question frames the discussion.**

The news media has lost credibility with many people. There has always been an appropriate place for commentary in the media. However, the balance is often tipped toward commentary and away from asking for input from "experts" on all sides of any issue. There is a dangerous shift away from interrogative influence, asking the hard questions.

When you ask questions, you aren't "preaching" at people. You are interacting with them. One of the reasons the press has come under scrutiny is that *they* ask all the questions. Even more, questions in search of truth should be neutral. There is a new trend to use questions that are prejudicially slanted.

Civil questions should not be "loaded." Loaded questions put leaders on the defensive. The questions frame the discussion. If someone asks you a question that makes you uncomfortable or you're not prepared to answer, *ask a question right back.* Reframe the conversation. Otherwise, you may be led in a direction you don't want to go. Remember, most issues lie in the territory of culture.

In the next chapter, we will look at how civil communication is respectful. It is Lesson #7.

Chapter Nine
The Art of Respectful Communication: Lesson #7

"I want no criticism of America at my table. The Americans criticize themselves more than enough."

— Winston Churchill[1]

Your communication with others carries more influence than you likely realize. You communicate in numerous ways—not just words from your mouth. The way you communicate can become a powerful engine to multiply positive respect.

Are you a respectful communicator? When you were a kid did you ever say the lie, "Sticks and stones may break my bones, but words can never hurt me?" What fool started that nonsense? The Bible says, "A word out of your mouth...can accomplish nearly anything—or destroy it!... It [can] set off a forest fire.... By our speech we can ruin the world, turn harmony to chaos, throw mud on a reputation, send the whole world up in smoke and go up in smoke with it, smoke right from the pit of hell."[2]

In the public media or in politics, those who teach or preach are responsible for *civil communication*. Civil communication is respectful communication. Free speech isn't free if it includes the price of losing the dignity of a

> **The level of communication is not a pretty sight.**

civilized society. This is the responsibility of every person. With electronic media, that responsibility has soared. For many, the level of communication is not a pretty sight. *It often seems human beings are smart enough to invent social technology, but not always wise enough to use it.* Perhaps you've heard this: "Keep your words soft and sweet. You never know when you'll have to eat them."[3] Could that apply to a whole nation? What about the whole world?

Six Dimensions of Respectful Communication

#1 What You Say

The first component of respectful communication is choosing *what you say*. It is the discipline of putting your brain in gear before opening your mouth, before texting, writing an email, or going on camera. Effective communicators don't simply analyze content. Respectful communication includes checking your compass. Don't fool yourself: Every time you open your mouth to speak, every time your thoughts are electronically multiplied, you are shaping, supporting, or undermining culture. You are influencing values, beliefs, attitudes, priorities, and worldviews. You are responsible to your nation, your world, and your Maker. Or...you are irresponsible.

As we covered in the previous chapter, on sensitive issues, it's often better to ask a question rather than make a statement. You can say, "Hey, Sally, I was thinking about the meeting we had this morning. Sometimes I think our boss is an idiot." A more respectful approach would be, "Hey, Sally, about that meeting this morning, what did you think about our boss's comments?"

#2 How You Say It

A second element of respectful communication is related: *how you say it.* In your speaking, even your reactions, do you add clarity or

> **In your speaking, do you add clarity or confusion?**

confusion? It seems as though, in national conversations, so many have added to the trash. Human beings are better than that. It is always an issue of respect. In Proverbs, the Bible says, "A gentle response diffuses anger, but a sharp tongue kindles a temper-fire."[4] Doesn't that make sense?

Consider what you hear and see from mass media, television, radio, films, etc. What people say communicates. So does the medium. If they are disrespectful, they send a cultural message. They lower the level of human dignity. When politicians share opposing views, it can be a learning process. However, when they frame their views in a disrespectful context, it reduces the *polite* dimension of *politics*. Those leaders influence you using an immoral ethic. You *can* disagree without being disagreeable. If you want to prove your point and help your cause, ignore the negative environment. Get a grip on reality. Use your compass. The medium sends a message, no matter what the content.

When I was in college, I worked summers at Ford Motor Company in their huge parts depot near Detroit. My boss, Pete, was a former NFL football player for the Chicago Bears. At nineteen, I was a little shocked by the work ethic of some of those on our midnight shift. I quickly learned why Pete had a bottle of Maalox on his desk. It seemed like something was always going wrong, particularly on the shipping dock. Of course, there was pressure: We had to get the parts shipped to the dealerships as fast as possible.

One night, a worker on the shipping dock ran a forklift through the side of the truck. Pete came down to the dock, cursing and yelling, throwing God's name around. I thought his behavior was disrespectful and undermined his authority. The next night, I went to his office to talk with him privately. Yeah, I was nervous.

Pete, can I have a few minutes of your time? Look, I know I'm just summer help, and I am really glad to have this job. I was just wondering, do you think all the bad language is necessary? I know some of these guys talk that way, but you are the boss and—I don't know—do you think they might respect you more if you didn't talk at their level?

Seriously? I thought my summer job would end that night! However, Pete began to tell me that he was a "lapsed Catholic" and knew better. He explained that his wife was seriously ill with cancer. He was under pressure from his boss because our shift was not meeting quotas. I just told him I would pray for him and for his wife, and I went back to work.

About a week later, we had another incident on the shipping dock. He came down and gathered our crew together. It was easy to see, he was justifiably angry. He let slip a couple of curse words, paused, looked right at me, and apologized! Later, I caught him alone and said, "Pete, you don't have to apologize to me. It's not about me. It's about you and your influence over our crew."

Pete changed his approach from that moment. The shipping department wasn't perfect, but it got better. He gained more respect. It improved his leadership. Every spring after that, Pete would call my mom: "Is Kent out of school yet? When will he be out? I'm holding a position open for him." It's true, I worked hard. However, you know what he did? He gave me every raise, at the earliest date allowed by the union. Respectful communication works—for everyone. Though it was not my intention, I gained Pete's respect. See how this works?

#3 Timing

Respectful communication is sensitive to *timing*. *When* you communicate is important. Good communication is an action, not a reaction. If you jump into the discussion in the heat of the moment, that *heat* transfers to your words. It steals your *light*. Your contribution becomes negative rather than positive. Civil communication is a discipline.

It takes effort to be a good *listener*. It takes more discipline to hear and understand than it takes to talk. If you are only "half listening," you are disrespectful.

> **If you are only "half listening," you are disrespectful.**

When I consult churches, I interview people, one on one, all day long, day after day. At the end of each day, I'm more exhausted than if I spoke to a large audience. Listening is hard work.

The timing of when you address an issue may require that you wait. It takes courage to be proactive rather than reactive. Sometimes, it is important just to say, "Let me think about that." You usually don't have to respond immediately.

#4 Choose the Medium

Respectful communication includes the disciplined pause you make to intentionally *choose the medium*. When someone sends you an email, it doesn't require that you respond by email. When was the last time you received an email charged with emotion, filled with sensitive issues? Here's how a civil person responds: Take charge. Don't let the email dictate the medium. You choose the medium. Break the misuse of the medium for the purpose of quality communication.

The right medium might be a phone call or face-to-face dialogue—not an email. Email is wonderful technology. It's great for limited, factual, non-emotional content...and not much more. Why? It can never become a conversation. An email doesn't convey tone of voice, emotion, empathy, or body language. An emotional e-mail is a "dump mechanism."

An email can easily be copied to countless others with the stroke of a key. If it's simply factual content, it's a great tool. If it's emotional, judgmental, critical, or accusatory, it is gossip. If you send an email that unloads damaging content to the recipient and copy it to others, that is slander. Since it is in writing, it is libel.

Every communication vehicle has its own strengths and weaknesses: telephone, texting, Instagram, television, radio, films, etc. Your choice of medium, purposefully exercised, is a reflection of your civility. As a parent, sometimes you can write a note to your child: "Don't forget to pack your lunch." With respectful communication, you may add more: "Don't forget to pack your lunch...have a great day...you're the best...I love you...see you tonight...we'll go out for pizza." You see, it's never "only a note." It's never "just" a sound bite, or "simply" a phone call or a text. Even punctuation in a text message can become stronger communication: "Love you," or "Love you!"

> **Words cast vision—for good or for bad.**

In the 2016 presidential election, Donald Trump's catchphrase was "Make America Great Again!" Hillary Clinton's phrase was "Better Together." These examples are not a Republican or a Democrat issue, or even about the people involved. On the issue of respectful communication, the phrase "Make America Great Again" focuses on the nation, the future, and a dream. The phrase "Better Together" focuses on "it's about you and me," or "let's huddle up." Words cast vision—for good or for bad.

Presidential candidates have large egos. That is a given for anyone who runs for the highest office in the land. It is also likely that a campaign worker or marketing group chose the phrases used by the two candidates. Focusing on the power of respect, what can you learn about communicating using your compass?

#5 Length of Communication

Respectful communication includes *how long you communicate*. One of the greatest contributors to my writing is my editor/friend Rob Olson. He is smart, blunt, and tough. He is a great friend, encourages my work, and is the first person who reads my manuscripts. Rob is tough, but loving. He loves short sentences and short paragraphs. Most of all, he is the best at what it means to be a critic. The word "critic" sometimes morphs to "criticism," which sounds negative. However, the word "critic" also means "careful." You can be a valuable critic for others without being critical in the negative sense.

I went to a workshop where the speaker began, "I came here to speak tonight. You came here to listen. If you get finished before I do, let me know!"[5] Perhaps you have followed the hearings conducted by politicians. How can these hearings drag on for months, and sometimes

> **You can be a valuable critic for others without being critical in the negative sense.**

years? When you communicate to others, take into account your "talk time." Respect others: their ability to listen and to comprehend.

#6 The Use of Story

Respectful communication uses the power of story, the subject of the previous chapter. Choose anyone in history you consider a great communicator. You likely identified a masterful storyteller. Consider Mark Twain. He could say paragraphs in eight words or less. Or Oliver Wendell Holmes. There are many who might come to mind. Good communicators animate using great stories.

Years ago, I read this story in a newsletter for ministers: The young preacher decided to start his career by delivering a fiery message to his new congregation. He began, "This sermon is about that small piece of flesh, the most dangerous appetence of a man's body." The men in church blanched. The women blushed, as he elaborated on all the horrendous consequences of its misuse, his piercing eyes shooting sparks as he expounded on and on. Toward the end of the sermon, he leaned over the pulpit and raised his voice. "Shall I name you that small piece of flesh?" The congregation was paralyzed in silence. He continued, "Shall I show you that small piece of flesh?" There were horrified gasps. The young preacher smiled and said, "Ladies and gentlemen, behold the small piece of flesh, the source of so many sins!" And he stuck out his tongue.[6] Enough said! Maybe too much!

Communication Power

There is power in stories, even the nursery rhymes you read to children. Communication is an engine of interaction. From creation, humans have this gift at a dramatically higher level than animals. People have an advanced form of communication. Humans, alone, write and read books. We share ideas, not simply by mimicking actions, but by advanced language and reasoning. This level of communication is a miraculous benefit...and an awesome challenge.

You have ideas. Your communication moves ideas forward.

> **Communication is a miraculous benefit...and an awesome challenge.**

The automotive leader Lee Iacocca once said, "You can have brilliant ideas, but if you can't get them across, your ideas won't get you anywhere."[7] How do you move your ideas forward to action? Are you respectful? If not, you are a bully.

The human gift of advanced communication comes with a serious responsibility. Words formed into ideas can be used for good or evil, for benefit or harm. If you watch, hear, or read the news, you know when communication is helpful or hurtful. Communication is both a privilege and a responsibility. That is why our Creator gave human beings the gift of communication balanced by the discipline of judgment. Polite, respectful people use good judgment. They understand: Words and ideas can help or hurt. With this power comes responsibility.

The Master, Jesus, said, "It's your heart, not the dictionary, that gives meaning to your words.... Words are powerful; take them seriously. Words can be your salvation. Words can also be your damnation."[8]

In our world today, words and ideas—with or without good judgment—are supercharged by enhanced delivery systems. Once in a while you'll hear

> **Words and ideas are supercharged by enhanced delivery systems.**

warnings, "Be careful about what you put online," or "Be cautious about what you tweet." In spite of those cautions, sometimes the rhetoric seems out of control. The end result becomes new levels of division, pessimism, and discouragement.

Unfortunately, it seems many have concluded that they don't require discipline of the tongue. It is easy to become so calloused we lose our civility. We are civilized people. Yet, some communicate in an uncivilized manner. Sometimes, it is better to keep your mouth shut and let people wonder if you are a fool rather than open it and remove all doubt.

Respectful communicators know that the carrot motivates, but the stick demotivates. You can be an encourager, or you can be a discourager. I know a woman whose parents created an environment with a negative, restrictive, overly cautious, judgmental worldview. It has taken their daughter years to overcome the negative influence of her parents' communication weaknesses. This raises the question: Where did her parents get it? They had to get it somewhere.

Attitudes and worldviews are usually caught and experienced, rather than simply taught. What about your background? Mark Twain said, "Keep away from people who belittle your ambitions. Small people always do that, but the really great people make you feel that you, too, can become great."[9] Respectful people are encouragers.

> **Respectful people are encouragers.**

Are you critical? Do you focus on what went wrong and say little about accomplishments? Are you known for what you are *against*, but others can't figure out what you are *for*? What about the newscasts on television? They are almost totally focused on the negative—the dark side of society. Shouldn't television news be split 50/50, with half of the reporting on what is right, good, and helpful? That sounds logical, since the majority of people do not steal, rape, or murder.

There are many people who report that their great achievements are the result of someone who thought "they could." Jesus told His followers they were ambassadors for God! He said you can pray for someone and miracles could result, through God's intervention. He said that He and His movement are the way, the truth, and the life—eternal life. He left the movement in the hands of His followers. Jesus said they could change the world. He told them to reach the whole world. And they are still working at it, twenty-one centuries later!

Will you be an encourager? William James said, "We should seize every opportunity to give encouragement. Encouragement is oxygen to the soul."[10] If you believe that, what is the oxygen level in your home? In your church? In your business? What about in Washington, D.C.—how is the oxygen level there? This is not political bias. This is a life bias. This is a future priority. This is a productivity engine. What about news outlets? Do the newspapers, magazines, and Hollywood films give you fresh, invigorating air to breathe? Zig Ziglar said, "Encouragement is the fuel of hope, and praise, particularly for effort, brings even more effort in the future."[11]

Your words are powerful—for good or for bad. Your tongue, your keyboard, your pen, your phone—they are all engines for interaction. They result in positive progress or discouraging, distractive disruption. In the Bible, there is a great proverb: "The right word at the right time is like a custom-made piece of jewelry; and a wise friend's timely reprimand is like a gold ring slipped on your finger."[12] Are you a respectful communicator?

Disrespectful Communication

Have you ever been faced with disrespectful communication? How did it leave you? For most, it's discouraging. How does that increase productivity? How does that mirror a civilized society? Do you remember? Dogs bark. People talk. While it is said, "A dog is a person's best friend," nobody really appreciates the barking. Some people love their dog, but communicate about others

> **Can you disagree without being disagreeable?**

as if they are the enemy. Can you disagree without being disagreeable? Can you work toward solutions, or are you part of the challenge?

When people talk past one another, it is a symbol of judgmental attitudes. However, there is a gift the Creator has given to humans: to seek understanding, through dialogue. How is that working for you? Do you spend more time judging or seeking to understand? Are you an encourager or a discourager? Anyone can look at people and see their weaknesses. It takes respect to see what they can become and encourage them to reach their potential. If you *encourage*, you speak courage into them. Who couldn't use a dose of that?

When you lose respect for someone, you run the risk of seeing everything about them from a negative perspective. You might generalize and condemn every little thing about them. Isn't that a form of prejudice, to take on a negative position toward another? How does that work out for you, as a human being? How does that impact the society? If you are prejudiced against someone of another ethnic group, you'll stir up a hornet's nest of reaction. But what about the personal prejudice of a news outlet, talk show host, politician, university professor, or celebrity? It is disrespectful!

No one is totally worthless. Everyone has some good qualities. When you are totally negative, you're wrong. You're prejudicial. You are a demagogue—one who stirs up people by appeals to emotions and prejudice in order to win them over quickly and gain power. How does that help?

A country can have the greatest military on the planet and still self-destruct from internal dry rot. You can create luxury automobiles, the latest technology, and have many people with advanced degrees— and still be uncivilized. You can boast of the greatest economy, the best inventions, the most powerful breakthroughs and still disintegrate through immoral disrespect toward one another. A nation can innovate and migrate into the future. Or it can disintegrate into history.

Your role in communication is not to impress people. It is to impact them. Your goal is not to simply prove your point to the next generation. It is to encourage, inspire, and inform them, for their good. Much of the toxiç rhetoric bombarding our world today originates from communicators who are entirely focused *on their own good* and their own cause. The goal is not dialogue toward meaning, but mean-spirited combat. It feels like the age of bullying. Can't you feel the coming implosion? Money can't buy a civilized society, at any price.

Great Communication

Anyone can make the simple difficult. But it takes a gifted person to make the difficult understandable. Great communicators make their mark on history. They are wordsmiths.

> **It takes a gifted person to make the difficult understandable.**

Their words communicate huge ideas. Consider the words of Aristotle, Jesus, Shakespeare, Lincoln, Churchill, King, and Graham. Agree with them or not, you know they got the point across. They inspired.

Early on in history, God addressed communication when he gave the commandments to the people of Israel. One of the Ten Commandments focused on speaking the truth to one another and being careful not to accuse another person falsely. Many centuries later, Jesus communicated God's love for every precious person. His respect for human beings was demonstrated in words and actions, no matter what it cost—even death. According to the Bible, "God is love...."[13] Most people have heard one of the most common sentences in Scripture: "This is how much God loved the world: He gave His Son, His one and only Son. And this is why: so that no one need be destroyed; by believing in Him, anyone can have a whole and lasting life."[14]

The above verse is followed by the posture of God—a good reminder about our posture toward one another. It says, "God didn't go to all the trouble of sending His Son merely to point an accusing finger, telling the world how bad it was. He came to help, to put the world right again."[15] What forms your communication approach? Are you known as an accusatory finger-pointer? Or, is your approach to help make the world right again? Some years after Jesus, one of his followers, Paul, wrote, "…speak the truth in love…."[16]

Recently, I visited a friend who loves to fish. On the wall of his "man cave" is a mounted largemouth bass. The words underneath read, "If I had kept my mouth shut, I wouldn't be here." Respect begins by being a good listener. When your kids are in their early years of learning to talk, sometimes they go on and on, and you're not sure where it's going. It's a test for every parent. This test, I've learned, is even more significant for a grandparent! What about when you have to listen to your neighbor's kids? A truly great person is also a respectful listener. There is a difference between hearing and active listening. Listening with intent is the art to discover meaning. It is your civil responsibility.

Meaning is the first step to understanding. Understanding leads to progress. Progress is the antidote to the roadblocks that plague society. We are overloaded with communication, but suffocating from gridlock. Many talk a lot. But work

> **Meaning is the first step to understanding.**

together for good? Not so much. Many are saturated with computer screen time, but can't communicate face to face.

Great citizens discuss ideas. Average citizens discuss events. Poor citizens discuss people. If you are a person who struggles achieving impact, it may be your primary focus is on yourself. Recently, we had a young staffer named Meghan. She recently married and moved to where her husband works. She left a note of thanks to me. It was a reminder about focus. Meghan wrote, "I learned a lot from you. When you enter a room, you greet everyone in the room." My thought was, "Of course, doesn't everyone do that?" In a civil society, others come first. The relative effectiveness of your communication skills depends on whether your worldview revolves around you or around others.

Ten Guidelines for Respectful Communication

1. Think before you speak, write, tweet, or blog—especially if you're upset.

2. Never listen to another person speak negatively about someone who is not present.

3. No matter how communication comes to you, STOP—THINK—DECIDE. What is the healthy way to respond? Choose the form of your response proactively. Never react by mimicking the way it came to you. Two wrongs don't make it right—they make it worse.

4. If someone offends you, follow Jesus' direction in the Bible (Matthew 18:15-17). (1) Go to the person and meet face to face. This does not mean asking them to meet you on your turf. It could mean a neutral site for both. (2) If you don't make progress, return a second time and take an objective, wise person with you. (3) If you still do not make progress, involve other wise leaders who are impartial. Focus on having a discussion, not a debate, argument, or power play.

5. When interacting with others, practice low control/high accountability. You don't make progress pushing people. If you can't respect the values of another person and move ahead for the greater good, you are the roadblock. Get help.

6. Do not avoid sensitive issues with the excuse that you don't like conflict. No normal, healthy person likes conflict. Life is not

always about doing what you "like." You can have convictions without acting like a convict.

7. Never provide a written copy, or share verbally with others, a disagreement issue you have with someone else. That is libel (written) and slander (verbal). Check out the ninth commandment in the Bible, in Exodus 20, a document that, for centuries, has helped people get along well.

8. Focus on charity when you have an issue with someone in authority. In a civil culture, you are to act with respect toward those who are in authority. This is a theme of the fifth commandment, which calls it a sin to disrespect those who are in authority. You can disagree without being disagreeable.

9. Do not publicly criticize others. Contact them privately. Focus on loving corrections, repentance, and forgiveness rather than public criticism, judgmentalism, and a spirit of self-righteousness. Pray for others who mess up. When you publicly criticize others, you undermine your own credibility. Those around you are mostly interested in what you are *for*, not what you are *against*. Being *for* something, even something different, is what respectful people do. Being *against* something or someone erodes your credibility. Everyone around you wants to know one thing: "What's your better plan?" Prove, with civility, why it's better.

10. As you speak the truth in love, start and end with appreciation for the positive. Don't avoid hard subjects, but surround them with identified positives. If you can't think of anything good about another person, then you are the person with the greater

issue—always.

If there is one word that describes the need to return to civility, it is *anger*. Think about mass shootings—in Las Vegas, in synagogues, and in schools. Hate and anger are evil cousins. Holding onto anger is like drinking poison and expecting the other person to die.[17]

> **One word describes the need to return to civility: anger.**

In Chapter Ten, we look at the great opportunity we have to refresh culture.

Chapter Ten
Refresh the Power of Culture

"Where do you think all these appalling wars and
quarrels come from? ...They come about because you
want your own way,... You're spoiled children, each
wanting your own way.... Say a quiet *yes* to God and
he'll be there in no time.... God is in charge of deciding
human destiny."

— James[1]

After speaking at a conference in California, I gathered a dozen retirees
and asked them to reflect on changes they have observed in our nation
over the years. I framed the discussion by talking about culture. I then
wrote on a whiteboard the elements of culture: values—what you
consider to be important; beliefs—what you demonstrate is truth;
attitudes—your posture toward life and the world; priorities—what you
almost always will do first; and worldviews—the way you see the world
and the way the world works.

In this conversation, I asked them to summarize their perception
of the quality of life in America right now, on a scale of 1 to 10, 1 being
very poor and 10 being excellent. When I got the scores and put them
together, they reported an average of 7.6. If you think about it, what
number would you give? What element of culture would rate higher?
What issues would score lower?

When I asked if they had experienced much change over the

years, the room exploded with conversation. Everyone agreed on several issues:

1. America is still a great place to live.
2. The culture, during their lifetime, has changed dramatically.
3. The quality of culture has eroded.
4. The quality of life is good, but not as good as it used to be.
5. The moral, peaceful, safe, joyful environment has declined.

Then I asked about the future. I used this diagnostic question: "What do you think it will be like for your grandchildren, fifteen to twenty years from now?" I asked them to rate this prediction about the quality of life on a scale of 1 to 10, 10 being excellent. The score, on average, was 4.5 for the grandchildren.

This is an exercise we have used with hundreds of people who have grandchildren younger than twelve years of age. The numbers are always lower than their own numbers. When we invite them to speculate why, the responses come quickly. They don't have to think about it. Why? They think about it often.

What preoccupies the thoughts of so many who have a more dismal picture in fifteen to twenty years, of a nation that they still feel is somewhat great? They talk about illegal drugs—some manufactured in this country and more coming illegally across the border. They speak about the increasing odds that their grandchildren could be killed in a school shooting. They sense the rising number of angry or troubled people who can make schools unsafe.

They say they don't believe the next generation will receive Social Security. They believe their grandchildren will work until they die just to make ends meet. At this point, they talk about government gridlock and the inability of leaders to accomplish much of anything that will improve our nation and our world. These comments are unsolicited. There are no leading questions. No matter who we interview, the concerns are remarkably similar.

We have been asking these questions for the last ten years, interviewing hundreds of people. The one and only credible summary of this sampling is that whatever the markers, even among younger adults, in their thirties and forties, the culture, by perception, is drifting in a negative direction. Overwhelmed by cultural deterioration, many people today are in a funk about the future. What would *you* say?

Hopeless

As hopelessness increases, receptivity toward meaningful change increases. Consider Israel, just before the birth of Christ. For centuries, the people lived

> As hopelessness increases, receptivity toward change increases.

with the promise that God would give them a land. From slavery in Egypt to wandering in the wilderness, they eventually landed in what would become Israel. They were also promised a Savior.

At the time Jesus was born, this promised land—promised by God Himself—was occupied by the Romans. In fact, most of the Mediterranean world was occupied by Roman soldiers. For the people of Israel, this was more than foreign occupation. This was, for them, against everything they believed about God and His promised land.

The Roman soldiers were fierce and feared. They used crucifixion—one of the most horrible, painful, and agonizing ways to kill someone. The Romans taxed the people in the countries they occupied. This was especially offensive to the people of Israel. Their worldview was that everything they owned—including money they earned—was a gift from God. Now, they were taxed to support a pagan emperor known for his immoral parties and killing people for sport.

The end result? The people of Israel were hopeless. So were those in the other occupied countries throughout that part of the world. Despair was everywhere. Everyone knew that no one could conquer Rome.

This is a historic lesson about despair. *Troubled people become receptive.* Why would God send the promised Savior right at the time when the promised land was occupied by Rome? Because the people were receptive. In fact, Christianity exploded with growth throughout the Mediterranean world during the first two centuries. Eventually, another emperor, Constantine, declared the Roman Empire "Christian."

Despair leads to hopelessness. Hopelessness generates receptivity. Receptivity becomes fertile ground for faith. Faith restores hope. This is why many say Jesus is "the hope of the world." It is why Peter wrote to Christians saying, "Be ready at all times to gently share the hope you have within you."[2]

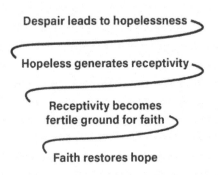

Despair leads to hopelessness

Hopeless generates receptivity

Receptivity becomes fertile ground for faith

Faith restores hope

Recently, I obtained a script of a popular American radio show host who was on the air from 1951 to 1953. Here is a paragraph from the script of the program:

[There is] disregard and disrespect for authority, hatred, revenge, and discrimination; lust; greed and dishonesty; gossip and slander; envy and jealousy, stressful discontent and obsessive selfishness. Isn't it time we all recognize the danger in the paganism that threatens to engulf us? The shift to pagan values in our society has crowded God and things spiritual farther and farther off stage. And we, with our little faith and lukewarm devotion, have probably done some pushing ourselves.[3]

So, what do you think? Do people, in every era, at a certain age, feel like the world is "going to the dogs"? Or, did the culture deteriorate as Reverend Oldsen described it in the early 1950s? Has it now drifted that much further? Is this simply a common worldview issue? Or is it a cultural issue?

It is interesting, however, to observe some of the resurgence of Christianity in the years following the 1950s. The Jesus Movement drew thousands of people, many of them younger. There was an explosion of worship songs written in contemporary language with style and instruments in the genre of that time. The Bible was being translated into contemporary language. Billy Graham was filling stadiums, speaking to thousands more on television and radio. Christian radio stations, playing contemporary Christian songs, began appearing across the landscape. Christian parachurch ministries were growing: Youth for Christ, InterVarsity, Campus Crusade, Youth With a Mission.

It is common for cycles of despair to generate new actions. Hopeless people become receptive. Pushed far enough, people "wake up" to spiritual realities. There is a realization: "We can't go on this way." There is receptivity to reexamine life at its most basic levels.

The big picture of environmental culture is complicated. Some issues are fads, part of the popular culture. Other issues are trends, which represent traditional values of culture. Clothing styles are popular culture issues (unless they get too risqué). Respect for life is a traditional value, a trend.

One issue is clear: You can do something about how you influence others. You do make a difference among those you touch. You do have responsibility in your civil role. You can be a champion for positive change. Do your Facebook page, Twitter account, conversation, and attitude reflect respect? Do your emails? Is your attitude respectful? In your thinking, your communication, your ideas and actions, would you dare ask the Creator and Ruler of the universe, "What do You think about me?" God has a whole volume of responses. It's called the Bible. It's not that God is silent on any or every subject that keeps you up at night. It's there, if you read it, if you listen. How important is that for your grandchildren?

What else is certain? Culture is subject to drift. It is constantly moving, like a second hand on a clock, one tick at a time. It's moved by people like you. It's a slow process. It's incremental.

> **Culture is subject to drift.**

Yet, it impacts everything. It implies that little events in your life do make a difference! It also implies the quality of cultural life can improve.

The Roman Empire didn't fall in a day, or even a year. So, what should get your attention? It absolutely self-destructed. But, you can do something about your culture. Cultural dimensions that add value to life can be increased—or greatly eroded—in one generation. You are on duty every day. It may be true that the great big world out there shapes us. It is also true that we shape it, one person at a time. That is the way it works.

Attrition and erosion occur in every dimension of culture. Review your last five years, personally. Where have you moved on values, beliefs, attitudes, priorities, and worldviews? Toward the positive or toward the negative? This is very personal. Take inventory on yourself.

Erosion and attrition occur all the time, sometimes dramatically. A daughter inherits the parents' business, but not their culture. The business begins to fail. Parents were active in a church, demonstrating a living faith. What about the children? They got the "religion," but not the faith. They attend church for weddings, funerals, and perhaps on holidays. But the culture of the Kingdom of Jesus? Not so much.

Politicians can drift from a culture that was built by the nation's founding fathers. Carl Sandburg said, "For we know when a nation goes down and never comes back, when a society or civilization perishes, one condition may always be found. They forgot where they came from. They lost sight of what brought them along."[4]

A film called *The Founder*[5] is about the cultural issues during the rise of McDonald's restaurants. It is a great study about values, beliefs, attitudes, priorities, and worldviews. The McDonald brothers had a great business at their restaurant in California. They not only mastered speed of delivery to their store window but also quality of food. Ray Kroc came along and, before they realized it, he changed the values. He changed the quality of the ice cream and some of the food. His value was building an empire and making millions of dollars, which he did. In the process, he changed the culture.

Ultimately, Ray Kroc overtook the McDonald brothers. His vision wasn't their vision. You could say his worldview was different. He developed the company into a franchise operation. The McDonald brothers' personal and relational commitment was gone forever. Ultimately, after some sad moments for the McDonalds, their ownership was bought out. They had wealth, but their "baby" had died. It is a story about money, success, and business savvy versus quality, relationships, integrity, and mission. What is that? Civility? Progress? Normal growth? Were the McDonald brothers "not minding the store"? Does it even matter? What if it was not about burgers, but your nation? Your life? The lives of your grandchildren?

One Nation

As a nation, the American ideals were built around some formulas: "United we stand, divided we fall" and "one nation under God." However, we have not always been united. In early American history, the country was bitterly divided by the Civil War and everything it represented. In the Vietnam era, the country was divided again, about the legitimacy of the war, the draft, and the cause. Today, the nation is strongly divided by values and beliefs that impact attitudes, priorities, and worldviews. The nation is divided by the "right" and the "left." The government is divided to the point of gridlock between Republicans and Democrats. Friends and families are divided as conservative and liberal.

As for "one nation under God," the American church, to a great extent, is floundering. To some degree, ineffective churches are complicit in the challenges facing America. Many congregations are rapidly declining. Some have watered down biblical teaching. Others are stuck in old strategies of obsolescence. Some have done both. The result is that many churches are positioned to fail. They will fail their communities. They will fail their God. They will fail their nation.

They can be "fixed"—yet, only if the people in those churches get help to return to biblical culture and replace ineffective, worn-out strategies. Only through renewal will congregations return to the culture of the Kingdom of God. Using adaptive strategies, they can move again toward effective impact.

Christian churches, faithful people, are more important to the nation's future than most of the media would ever imagine. They can restore hope to America. When churches respect God and the Bible, they will foster respect among Americans. Some churches are growing, impacting lives today. However, many are declining. Even faith is divided.

There were crosses on the sails of the Mayflower for a reason. Those pilgrims were on a mission "for the glory

> **Those pilgrims were on a mission.**

of God, and advancement of the Christian faith...."[6] It was their mission, according to the *Mayflower Compact*. What is the "American Compact" today? Does anyone remember our roots—what got us here?

Where Do We Stand?

What are our values? What is our mission and our purpose today? For what great purpose do we strive? Are these, actually, the UNITED States? Do we have a common worldview? Are we clear about our priorities? Or, has the level of civility become a fog of dysfunction? These are serious issues for every person. Can we tolerate being the silent majority any longer? Can we rise above the fog and return to the platform of respect that allows us to constructively discuss, learn, grow, and move forward? Can this become a defining moment in history? If we think it's impossible, we have already buried our future.

The role of civility is significant. Out of turmoil, respectful people with strong convictions emerge. It is a cycle civilized human beings repeat. Today, there are some positive signs that those following the compass may be emerging in every sector of our society. It seems that, in every generation, basic lessons must be relearned, passion reignited, culture rebooted. The cultural direction can be rediscovered, reset, and refreshed. No matter how discouraged you are, life can improve. Cultural architects rebuild. Are you one of them? Of course you are. Will you rise to this occasion? That is up to you. There is more at stake than you likely imagine.

Culture Compass

In the process of rebuilding respect, the cultural compass is absolutely essential. Civility is clarified by clear values, beliefs, attitudes, priorities, and worldviews. For a healthy society, a strong and unified commitment to culture provides the glue that allows great diversity of strategies.

> **Culture provides the glue that allows great diversity of strategies.**

A football team consists of athletes who have diverse roles. Some are on offense; others play defense. A few are kickers. Some are guards, others are tackles, and some are running backs. Diversity wins. But it is not everything. The team must be unified: Which direction are they going down the field? They share a commitment to follow their assignments, as plays are called by the coach. They agree to begin their assignment when the ball is snapped. They agree to continue their assignment until the whistle blows. They are united in their diversity.

A football team is doomed for failure without respect. That includes respect for the diversity. However, it also requires respect for the coaches, the quarterback, and the rules of the game. Without that respect, there is no team. Without respect, they lose.

For many people, the elements of healthy culture are present. There may be some who are a little fuzzy. They may be preoccupied with the challenges of life. Others have difficulty with focus. The compass of culture is deep inside. The direction is there, just somewhat distant. Have you taken time to clearly focus on your values? Are you clear about your beliefs? Can you describe your attitude about life? Have you clarified your priorities? Are you focused on what is most important? How do you understand your world and where you fit? How much does your compass guide your direction? Your behavior? Your purpose? Do you have hope?

Your Time

There is hope on the horizon. Why? The circle of culture continues to turn. Like the seasons of weather or the seasons of life, spring is on the horizon. Your alarm is inside. After so much backstabbing, leadership gridlock, so many shootings, suicides, addictions, broken families, damaged children, inflammatory talk, and disrespectful behavior, there comes a wake-up call. It's not a shout. No one yells. It's a quiet voice that speaks to your soul. You, on your watch, will not let your nation go down the toilet.

This is the season to refocus. Take a long, hard look at your cultural compass. Don't just react to your world. Sort out your values, beliefs, attitudes, priorities, and worldviews. Dig down deep inside. Look at yourself in the mirror. Who do you see? What do you see? What do you really want? What is your vision? Rediscover who you *really* are. Articulate the best of your culture to others. Look to your Creator. Don't be shy. Be you!

Discipline yourself. Translate your culture into action. Be proactive. Don't get up in the morning and wonder, "What will

> **You are on a mission of influence.**

happen today?" You are on a mission of influence. Don't lie on your couch and fret about those you can't change. Get on your feet and encourage those you can. If you want to be remembered as a great ancestor, it starts today.

Don't relive or rehash what happened back whenever. Change your thinking and let your compass empower your action. Mahatma Gandhi said, "Our greatness lies not so much in being able to remake the world as in being able to remake ourselves."[7]

Clearly define your purpose. You are a cultural architect. You shape others. You are on a mission. You are a dealer in hope. You shape history. You are an ambassador to the people of your land, and more: to the world.

Whoever you are, whatever you do, if you don't get culture right, you don't have a compass. If you don't have a cultural compass, you're lost in your own woods. You are not on a mission; you're out for a walk. If you use the compass of popularity, you draw circles—you miss the path for which you were born. You should not let this happen. There is far too much at stake!

The future is at stake. Lives are at stake, because if you don't help stop the shooters, somebody dies. If you don't help clean up the drugs, somebody dies. If you don't clarify culture, your nation dies. If you ignore your faith, you die. If you don't infuse your children with culture, they get lost. They lose. You lose. We all lose. The world loses.

You aren't signed up on a contract. You don't just influence until you retire. You aren't simply investing in your children until they leave home. You don't live in a vacuum. The seeds you nurture, the crops you tend, impact generations long after your name is forgotten. This is your legacy. Don't cut yourself short!

You can outlive your heirs and even your friends. There won't

> **Without legacy, no one knows why you lived at all.**

be many at your funeral, but your legacy demonstrates victory. You can die young and have a funeral crowded with people, but without legacy, no one knows why you lived at all. Don't get totally focused on making a living and fail to make a difference. A "difference" is not a pile of money you can't take with you or real estate your kids have to sell or a garage full of junk. A "difference" has only one container: human beings. You are the difference. You can't escape it.

You just decide: good or bad difference? It's your call.

Jesus started the largest, longest-lasting movement in history. His mission could have been to drive the Romans out of Israel. He would have been very popular. He would have enjoyed success, but not significance. If Jesus would have focused on the Romans, He would have been forgotten in 500 years. Even some churches that bear His name have lost the uniqueness and vision of His mission. The result is their decline and ultimate death.

Jesus' mission was to change people from themselves. His goal was to reclaim what people were created to be. He launched a movement: people embedded with love, forgiveness, peace. And this promise: His followers are with him for eternity. Many Christians and their churches mess it up—frequently. Yet, culture is so strong, forgiveness is so sure, restoration is so powerful, the movement is always refueled and revived. Civility is attractive.

A Civil Culture

In 1863, President Abraham Lincoln proclaimed March 30 to be a national day of fasting, humility, and prayer. He declared:

We have been the recipients of the choicest bounties of heaven. We have been preserved, these many years, in peace and prosperity. We have grown in numbers, wealth and power, as no other nation has ever grown. But we have forgotten God. We have forgotten the gracious hand which preserved us in peace, and multiplied and enriched and strengthened

186

us; and we have vainly imagined, in the deceitfulness of our hearts, that all these blessings were produced by some superior wisdom and virtue of our own. Intoxicated with unbroken success, we have become too self-sufficient to feel the necessity of redeeming and preserving grace, too proud to pray to the God who made us! It behooves us, then, to humble ourselves before the offended Power to confess our national sins, and to pray for clemency and forgiveness.[8]

If, in the busy sprint of life, you forget the basics, misplace your foundation, lose sight of your core, or wander from what makes you great, take out a penny—the most  fundamental element of the currency that reflects your crystallized sweat. Look at the front. You will see President Lincoln. That is your *heritage*. Look at the top. It says, "In God We Trust." That is your *hope*. Look to the left. It says, "Liberty." That is your *gift*. Look at the back. It begins, "United." That requires *civility*.

> **Your greatest achievement is who you are and who you become.**

The call for civility is not new. It is a recurring cycle. Your greatest achievement is who you are and who you become. Culture doesn't live in a constitution, in bylaws, or in a plaque on the wall. Not even on the currency. Culture lives in people like you. People impact people.

The City of Utilidor

Have you ever been to the city of Utilidor in Florida? Have you ever been near it? No? Have you ever been to Disney World? If so, you have been within fifty to one hundred feet of Utilidor. Very few people get the privilege of visiting that city. It is literally a city—*underneath* Walt Disney World.

Some years ago, I spoke at a conference in Epcot. As a benefit, I was led on an amazing tour of Utilidor: streets, shops, laundromats, garbage trucks, Brinks trucks, food for the workers—a real city! From my perspective, the highlight was the message at the entrance of Utilidor: "You can dream, create, design, and build the most wonderful place in the world, but it takes people to make the dream a reality."[9]

People are the world's most valuable asset. People are what culture is all about. They are our most valuable resource. You should focus more on God's most valuable creation: people. Great people grow great families. Great people build great companies—of great people. Great teachers inspire great students. Great workers do great work. Great people make great nations. Civility—respect—is respect for people. God has unfathomable respect for you! Great people have respect for God.

If you haven't before, you should take a serious look at Jesus. Don't just focus on His incredible life. Consider His spiritual claims. If you have wandered, wander back. With that focus, you will catch civility: respect with grace and forgiveness. You will learn to love others for who they are. You can learn to love yourself—even to forgive yourself.

There are positive results that come with following Jesus. One

of them is not human perfection. The real
result is forgiveness and restoration. Not just
for your past—every day. The results are

> **Forgiven and forgiving people can run a country.**

more love, joy, peace, patience, kindness, goodness, faithfulness,
gentleness, and self-control.[10] Do you think those results might help
everyone show more respect? Perfect people can't run a country—there
aren't any. Imperfect people can't run a country—they're too self-
centered. Forgiven and forgiving people can run a country, and run it
well.

If you are already a follower of Jesus, when people look at you,
do they see Jesus? Do they see Jesus' culture? Do they see the Kingdom
of God? Do they see the Kingdom in action? Do they experience respect
from you? Just because you call yourself a Christian doesn't mean you
can't grow into more of His culture.

It is not hard to imagine that Jesus weeps over lost opportunities
to extend His perfect love to imperfect people. It can happen— to you,
me, everyone—if we would simply get out of His way. This is your
primary mission. God is pleading for people, like you, who will refresh
the culture with His culture. God is pleading for people, like you, who
will refresh the culture of a nation that has so much that is good. We are
so close! Your respect for God is your greatest gift. Your respect for
others is your greatest contribution.

Acknowledgments

My commitment to excellence for every literary work requires a team effort. I'm grateful for those who helped make this book more impactful for you, the reader.

Thank you to our early reviewers for their critical input: Mark Sattler, Paul Stratton, Tom Koerner, Rob Olson, Steve Peterson, Bob Shriner, and Bob Probst. I am especially thankful to our team leader, Tracee Swank, for her guidance and encouragement. Also, words will never be enough to describe the amazing support for this project from my wife, Janet.

I am indebted to our Church Doctor Board members, who oversee our efforts to help churches and Christians to become more effective for changing the world: Greg Ulmer, Mark Welty, Mike Travers, Mark Sattler, and Steve Peterson.

Special thanks goes to the Church Doctor staff: Chelsey Strickler, Wendy Zolman, Jason Atkinson, Beth Knoll, Michele Ellison, Meghan Gjeltema, Matt Genszler, Jon Hunter, John Wargowsky, Andrew Carter, and Sarah Kolb.

We offer our deepest gratitude to Chris Blair for his efforts, input, and encouragement not only for this project but for his contributions to our ministry team. We were blessed by Chris' dedication and his gift to bring out the best in everyone and everything he came in contact with. We miss you, Chris, but rejoice in knowing we will see you again in heaven. We will do our best to continue to bring out the greater excellence in all those we serve.

It is a privilege to partner with Greg Johnson, leader of WordServe Literary Agency. Thank you for your ongoing wisdom and guidance.

It is an honor and privilege for all of us to invest in the readers of this book. Our greatest hope is that this effort will improve your life as you interact with others.

Endnotes

Introduction

1. Winston Churchill's last speech to the British House of Commons, March 1, 1955 taken from *Churchill in "Quotes": Wit and Wisdom from the Great Statesman.* East Sussex, United Kingdom: Ammonite Press, 2011, p. 158.
2. Matthew 24:12. *New International Version Bible,* Colorado Springs, CO: Biblica, Inc., 2011.
3. Hunter, Kent R., with Tracee J. Swank. *Who Broke My Church? 7 Proven Strategies for Renewal and Revival.* New York, NY: Hachette Book Group/FaithWords, 2017.
4. "Ask Not What Your Country Can Do for You (Kennedy's Inaugural Address)." Ushistory.org. Accessed January 14, 2019. http://www.ushistory.org/documents/ask-not.htm.
5. Frimer, Jeremy A., Skitka, Linda J. "The Montagu Principle: Incivility decreases politicians' public approval, even with their political base." *Journal of Personality and Social Psychology,* Vol. 115(5), Nov. 2018, pp. 845-866.
6. "The Persistent Passion of Vice President Mike Pence." by Philip Elliott. *Time Magazine.* June 5, 2017, p. 18.
7. www.britannica.com/topic/Mayflower-Compact [Emphasis mine].
8. Galatians 5:22-23. *The Message: The Bible in Contemporary Language.* Colorado Springs, CO: NavPress, 2002.

Chapter One

Behavior 101

1. 1 Peter 2:17. *The Message: The Bible in Contemporary Language.* Colorado Springs, CO: NavPress, 2002.
2. Burkus, David. "A Tale of Two Cultures: Why Culture Trumps Core Values in Building Ethical Organizations." *Journal of Values Based Leadership:* Vol. 4, No. 1 (Winter-Spring 2011). www.valuesbasedleadershipjournal.com / issues/ vol4issue1/ tale_2culture.php.
3. Spring Arbor University, Spring Arbor, MI. www.arbor.edu.
4. Ralph Waldo Emerson, quoted by Joseph Grenny, Kerry Patterson, David Maxfield, Ron McMillan, L. Switzler in *Influencer: The New Science of Leading Change.* New York, NY: McGraw Hill, 2013, p. 67.
5. 1 Corinthians 13:1. *The Message: The Bible in Contemporary Language.* Colorado Springs, CO: NavPress, 2002.

6. Steve Ballmer, CEO, Microsoft in *Fortune* magazine. https://fortune.com.
7. Jim Collins, speaker at the Global Leadership Summit, August 5, 2010.
8. 1 John 4:8. *New International Version Bible*, Biblica, Inc., 2011.
9. L. Bennett, *What Manner of Man* quoted by Burt Nanus. *Visionary Leadership: Creating a Compelling Sense of Direction for Your Organization.* San Francisco, CA: Jossey-Bass, 1995, pp. 138-139.
10. 1 Peter: 2:14. *The Message: The Bible in Contemporary Language.* Colorado Springs, CO: NavPress, 2002.
11. 1 Peter 3:8-12 (quoting Psalm 34:12-16). *The Message: The Bible in Contemporary Language.* Colorado Springs, CO: NavPress, 2002.
12. Gladwell, Malcolm. *The Tipping Point How Little Things Can Make a Big Difference.* New York, NY: Little, Brown and Company, 2000, p. 11.
13. This concept is expanded from the book *Thinking for a Change* by John C. Maxwell. New York: Time Warner Book Group (now Hachette Book Group), 2003, p. 38.
14. Stein, Jean. "William Faulkner, The Art of Fiction No. 12." *The Paris Review.* Issue 12, Spring 1956.
15. John C. Maxwell, Maximum Impact Club CD, "Decisions that Shaped My Life," Vol. 17, #10.
16. Leighton Ford, *Decision* Magazine, February 1976.
17. Matthew 19:16, 25b-26. *The Message: The Bible in Contemporary Language.* Colorado Springs, CO: NavPress, 2002.
18. Mother Teresa quoted by Darrow Miller. *Discipling Nations: The Power of Truth to Transform Cultures.* Seattle, WA: YWAM Pub., 2001, p. 236.

Chapter Two

The Master of Civility

1. John 15:16-17. *Good News Bible: The Bible in Today's English Version.* New York: American Bible Society, 1976.
2. Quote commonly attributed to Thomas Jefferson.
3. Ephesians 4:15. *Revised Standard Version of the Bible.* Division of Christian Education of the National Council of the Churches of Christ in the United States of America, 1971.
4. Thoreau, Henry David. *Walden.* Lexington, KY: CreateSpace, 2017, p. 98.
5. John 3:16-17. *The Message: The Bible in Contemporary Language.* Colorado Springs, CO: NavPress, 2002.
6. Barna, George. *Think Like Jesus: Make the Right Decisions Every Time,* Brentwood, TN: Integrity Publishers, 2003, p. 27.
7. Romans 12:1-2. *The Message: The Bible in Contemporary Language.* Colorado Springs, CO: NavPress, 2002.
8. John C. Maxwell, *How Successful People Think,* New York, NY: Hachette Book Group, 2009, introduction: IX-X, [Adapted].
9. *Les Misérables*, Universal Pictures, 2012.

10. Socrates quoted in *Leadership* magazine, Winter 1997, p. 75.
11. Rae Lynn Schleif, District Superintendent, Maumee Watershed District, Western Ohio Conference of the United Methodist Church, quoting Bishop Mtambo.
12. I have expanded these five elements at length in my book *Who Broke My Church? 7 Proven Strategies for Renewal and Revival*. New York, NY: Hachette Book Group/FaithWords, 2017.
13. Goethe quoted in Bill Capodagli and Lynn Jackson's book *The Disney Way: Harnessing the Management Secrets of Disney in Your Company*. New York, NY: McGraw-Hill, 2007, p. 53.
14. John 14:6a. *Good News Bible: The Bible in Todays' English Version*. New York: American Bible Society, 1976.

Chapter Three

The Infectious Principle: Lesson #1

1. Unknown origin, a common saying.
2. www.thesendmovement.com
3. Matthew 18:21-22. *Holy Bible,* New Living Translation. Carol Stream, IL: Tyndale House Publishers, Inc., 1996.
4. John 8:3-11. *The Message: The Bible in Contemporary Language*. Colorado Springs, CO: NavPress, 2002 [Paraphrase mine].
5. Leo Tolstoy, quoted by John C. Maxwell, *Living At The Next Level: Insights for Reaching Your Dreams*. Nashville, TN: T. Nelson Publishers, 1996, p. 90.
6. Howard Hendricks, quoted by John C. Maxwell, *It's Just a Thought—But It Could Change Your Life: Life's Little Lessons on Leadership*. Tulsa, OK: Honor Books, 1996.
7. 2 Corinthians 10:3-5. *The Message: The Bible in Contemporary Language*. Colorado Springs, CO: NavPress, 2002.
8. David Gurgen, Global Leadership Summit, 2009.
9. I'm grateful to my friend, Elmer Towns, co-founder of Liberty University, for this great insight.
10. Ford, Henry and Samuel Crowther. *My Life and Work*. New York, NY: Garden City Publishing Company, Inc., 1922, p. 72.
11. Matthew 28:19-20. *Holy Bible*, New Living Translation. Carol Stream, IL: Tyndale House Publishers, Inc., 1996.
12. Jim Collins, quoted by John C. Maxwell, Maximum Impact Club, The "3 G Leader"—part 1, Vol. 18, No. 2.

Chapter Four

Don't Settle for Success: Lesson #2

1. Shaw, George Bernard, Dan H. Laurence, and Stanley Weintraub. *Man and Superman: A Comedy and a Philosophy*. London, England: Penguin Books, 2004, p. xxxii.
2. Rustenbach, Rusty. "Giving Yourself Away." *Discipleship Journal*, March/April 1985.
3. Warren, Rick. *The Purpose Driven Life: What on Earth Am I Here For?* Grand Rapids, MI: Zondervan, 2005, p. 233.
4. Tom Manthei, quoted by Ben and Ruth Manthei, *In His Majesty's Service: From Success to Significance*. Charlevoix, MI: Creative Cottage Publishing Partnership, 2002, p. 31.
5. Bayrs, George (editor). *The Letters of John Wesley*. London, UK: Hodder & Stoughton, 1915, p. 423.
6. 1 John 4:16. *New International Version Bible*, Colorado Springs, CO: Biblica, Inc., 2011.
7. 1 John 4:19. *New International Version Bible*, Colorado Springs, CO: Biblica, Inc., 2011.
8. John C. Maxwell, Maximum Impact Audio Resource, Vol. 11, No. 5.
9. Acts 2:17-18. *The Message: The Bible in Contemporary Language*. Colorado Springs, CO: NavPress, 2002.
10. Manthei, Ben and Ruth Manthei, *In His Majesty's Service: From Success to Significance*. Charlevoix, MI: Creative Cottage Publishing Partnership, 2002, p. 32.
11. A comment shared with the author by Mark Marxhausen, from John Mason's book *Conquering an Enemy Called Average*. Tulsa, OK: Insight International, 1996.
12. Romans 12:1-2. *Revised Standard Version of the Bible*. Division of Christian Education of the National Council of the Churches of Christ in the United States of America, 1971.
13. Galatians 3:28. *Revised Standard Version of the Bible*. Division of Christian Education of the National Council of the Churches of Christ in the United States of America, 1971.
14. Hebrews 12:2. *Revised Standard Version of the Bible*. Division of Christian Education of the National Council of the Churches of Christ in the United States of America, 1971 [Emphasis mine].

Chapter Five

Hard to Be Humble: Lesson #3

1. Quote attributed to Napoleon Hill.
2. Collins, Jim C. *Good to Great: Why Some Companies Make the Leap ... and Others Don't*. New York, NY: Harper Collins, 2009, p. 30.

ENDNOTES

3. Furtick, Steven. *Sun Stand Still.* Colorado Springs, CO: Multnomah Books, 2018, p. 67.
4. 1 Corinthians 8:1-3. *The Message: The Bible in Contemporary Language.* Colorado Springs, CO: NavPress, 2002.
5. Proverbs 28:26. *The Message: The Bible in Contemporary Language.* Colorado Springs, CO: NavPress, 2002.
6. Matthew 7:1-3. *The Message: The Bible in Contemporary Language.* Colorado Springs, CO: NavPress, 2002.
7. Ephesians 4:15. *Holy Bible,* New Living Translation. Carol Stream, IL: Tyndale House Publishers, Inc., 1996.
8. Matthew 6:12. *Holy Bible,* New Living Translation. Carol Stream, IL: Tyndale House Publishers, Inc., 1996.
9. Warren, Rick. *The Purpose Driven Life: What On Earth Am I Here For?* Grand Rapids, MI: Zondervan, 2005, p.148.
10. Toffler, Alvin. *Future Shock.* New York, NY: Bantam Books, 1980, p. 414.
11. The preamble, *The Constitution of The United States of America,* 1788.
12. Abraham Lincoln quoted by Johan Engelbrecht, *Cherish the Dream: A Challenge to America to Reclaim Her Greatness.* Columbus, GA: TEC Publications, 2004, p. 64.
13. Gandhi, Mahatma. *The Collected Works of Mahatma Gandhi.* New Delhi, India: Publications Division, Ministry of Information & Broadcasting, 1999, pp. 133-134.
14. Abraham Lincoln's 1858 Senatorial Speech, debating Senator Stephen Douglas.
15. Duff, Sir Mountstuart E. Grant. *Notes from a Diary 1851-1872, Vol. I.* London, UK: John Murray, 1897, p. 237.
16. Matthew 18:20. *Revised Standard Version of the Bible.* Division of Christian Education of the National Council of the Churches of Christ in the United States of America, 1971.
17. Warren, Rick. *The Purpose Driven Life: What On Earth Am I Here For?* Grand Rapids, MI: Zondervan, 2005, p. 270.

Chapter Six

Organic Living: Lesson #4

1. Kinnaman, David and Gabe Lyons. *unChristian: What a New Generation Really Thinks about Christianity…and Why It Matters.* Grand Rapids, MI: Baker Books, 2007, p. 106.
2. Peters, George W. *A Biblical Theology of Missions.* Chicago, IL: Moody Press, 1984, p. 211.
3. Pierce, Chuck D. and Rebecca Wagner Sytsema, *The Future War of the Church.* Ventura, CA: Regal Books, 2007, p. 38.

4. Matthew 28:19-20 [Paraphrase mine].
5. Brierley, Peter. *God's Questions*. Tonbridge, Kent, UK: ADBC Publishers, 2010, p. 94.
6. Collins, Jim. *Good to Great*. New York, NY: HarperCollins Publishers Inc., 2001, p. 17.
7. Brafman, Ori and Rod A. Beckstrom. *The Starfish and the Spider: The Unstoppable Power of Leaderless Organizations*. London, England: Penguin Group, 2006, p.155.
8. Maxwell, John C. *Thinking for a Change*. New York, NY: Time Warner Book Group, 2003, p. 6 [Adapted].
9. Matthew 16:18. *New American Standard Bible*. La Habra, CA: The Lockman Foundation, 1995.
10. Rainer, Thom S. and Eric Geiger. *Simple Church: Returning to God's Process for Making Disciples*. Nashville, TN: B&H Publishing Group, 2006, pp. 84-85 [Adapted].
11. Kaiser, John Edmund. *Winning on Purpose: How to Organize Congregations to Succeed in Their Mission*. Nashville, TN, Abingdon Press, 2006, p. 61 (Adapted).
12. Hughes, Emmet John. *The Ordeal of Power: A Political Memoir of the Eisenhower Years*. New York, NY: Athenaeum, 1963, p. 124.
13. Engelbrecht, Johan. *Cherish the Dream: A Challenge to America to Reclaim Her Greatness*. Columbus, GA: TEC Publications, 2004, p. 29.

Chapter Seven

Four Ways to Build Respect: Lesson #5

1. Borthwick, Paul. *Six Dangerous Questions*. Downers Grove, IL: InterVarsity Press, 1996, p. 62.
2. Colossians 4:6. *The Message: The Bible in Contemporary Language*. Colorado Springs, CO: NavPress, 2002.
3. 1 Thessalonians 5:11. *Revised Standard Version of the Bible*. Division of Christian Education of the National Council of Churches of Christ in the United States of America, 1971.
4. Dr. Henry Cloud, Global Leadership Summit, August 8-9, 2013.
5. 1 Peter 4:1-3. *The Message: The Bible in Contemporary Language*. Colorado Springs, CO: NavPress, 2002 (emphasis mine).
6. Proverbs 29:18. *King James Version of the Bible*, public domain.
7. Proverbs 29:18. *New International Version Bible*, Colorado Springs, CO: Biblica, Inc., 2011.
8. Sanders, J. Oswald. *Spiritual Leadership: Principles of Excellence for Every Believer*. Chicago, IL: Moody Publishers, 2007, p. 57.
9. Quote attributed to Helen Keller.
10. *Net Results*, Vol. XVI, No. 6, June 1995.

ENDNOTES

11. Maxwell, John C. *Today Matters: Twelve Daily Practices to Guarantee Tomorrow's Success*, Center Street. New York, NY: Hachette Book Group, USA, 2004, p. 266.
12. Quote attributed to Blaise Pascal. www.goodreads.com
13. Kallestad, Walther P. *Wake Up Your Dreams: A Proven Strategy to Help You Discover Your Lifelong Dream, Make Dream Days a Regular Part of Your Life, Avoid Dream Danger Zones, Succeed by Finding a Dream Partner*. Grand Rapids, MI: Zondervan Publishing House, 1996, p. 156.
14. Matthew 5:13. *The Message: The Bible in Contemporary Language*. Colorado Springs, CO: NavPress, 2002.
15. Matthew 18:15-17. [Summary mine].
16. Romans 16:16. *Revised Standard Version of the Bible*. Division of Christian Education of the National Council of the Churches of Christ in the United States of America, 1971.

Chapter Eight

The Power of Story: Lesson #6

1. Miller, Donald. *Building a StoryBrand: Clarify Your Message So Customers Will Listen*. New York, NY: HarperCollins Leadership, 2017, p. 15.
2. Tim Costello, quoted by Neil Cole. *Organic Church: Growing Faith Where Life Happens*. San Francisco, CA: Jossey-Bass, 2005, p. 123.
3. Ed Catmull, CEO, Pixar, The Global Leadership Summit, August 6, 2015.
4. John Kotter quoted by Joseph Greeny, Kerry Patterson, David Maxfield, Ron McMillan, Al Switzler. *Influencer: The New Science of Leading Change*. VitalSmarts, 2013, p. 101.
5. Ralph Waldo Emerson quoted in Thom S. Rainer and Eric Geiger, *Simple Church: Returning to God's Process for Making Disciples*. Nashville, TN: B&H Publishing Group, 2006, p. 29.
6. Woodrow Wilson quoted by Zig Ziglar, *Staying Up, Up, Up in a Down, Down World: Daily Hope for the Daily Grind*. Nashville, TN: Thomas Nelson, 2004, p. 7.
7. Pope John Paul II, *Leadership* Magazine, Spring 1999.
8. Minneapolis Star-Tribune. 1-17-1998, by Judy Zmerold.
9. Kennedy, John F. "Address in the Assembly Hall at the Paulskirche in Frankfurt, Germany (266)," June 25, 1963, *Public Papers of the Presidents*: John F. Kennedy, 1963. https:// www. jfklibrary. org/ Research/Research-Aids/Ready-Reference/ JFK-Quotations.aspx.
10. Jay, Antony. *Lend Me Your Ears: Oxford Dictionary of Political Quotations* (Fourth Edition). New York, NY: Oxford University Press, 2010, p. 187.

11. Churchill, Winston. First speech as Prime Minister, House of Commons, 13 May, 1940.
12. Mandela, Nelson. www.forbes.com/sites/mfonobongnsehe/2013/12/06/20—inspirational—quotes—from—nelson—mandela.
13. Matthew 13:10-14. *The Message: The Bible in Contemporary Language.* Colorado Springs, CO: NavPress, 2002 [Emphasis mine].
14. Acts 1:8. [Summary mine].
15. I referenced President Trump's Twitter feed briefly in Chapter Three and the connection to the "infectious principle." Here, the focus is on the use of stories.
16. Miller, Darrow L. and Stan Guthrie. *Discipling Nations: The Power of Truth to Transform Cultures.* Seattle, WA: YWAM Publishing, 2001, p. 222.
17. The back of a toilet seat on a Virgin Atlantic train from Sheffield to London, England, January 27, 2016.
18. Sherman, Richard M. and Robert B. Sherman, composers. "A Spoonful of Sugar." (Performed by Julie Andrews in *Mary Poppins*). © Walt Disney Records, 1964.
19. St. Augustine of Hippo. *Confessions of St. Augustine.* Book 11, Chapter 12.
20. Matthew 16:13-16. *The Message: The Bible in Contemporary Language.* Colorado Springs, CO. NavPress, 2002.

Chapter Nine

The Art of Respectful Communication: Lesson #7

1. Churchill, Sir Winston. Meeting with Winthrop W. Aldrich, U.S. Ambassador-designate, November 30, 1955 taken from *Churchill in "Quotes": Wit and Wisdom from the Great Statesman.* East Sussex, United Kingdom: Ammonite Press, 2011, p. 162.
2. James 3:4-6. *The Message: The Bible in Contemporary Language.* Colorado Springs, CO: NavPress, 2002.
3. Quote attributed to Osborn Elliott.
4. Proverbs 15:1. *The Message: The Bible in Contemporary Language.* Colorado Springs, CO: NavPress, 2002.
5. Heard by the author at a conference led by Rev. Paul Foust, April 1975.
6. "Cross-Currents." *Seminex Vicarage Newsletter*, March 1977.
7. Quote commonly attributed to Lee Iacocca.
8. Matthew 12:34-37. *The Message: The Bible in Contemporary Language.* Colorado Springs, CO: NavPress, 2002.
9. Quote commonly attributed to Mark Twain.

ENDNOTES

10. *God's Little Instruction Book for New Believers*. Tulsa, OK: Honor Books, 1996, p. 128.
11. Ziglar, Zig. *Staying Up, Up, Up in a Down, Down World: Daily Hope for the Daily Grind*. Nashville, TN: Thomas Nelson Publishers, 2000, p. 162.
12. Proverbs 25:11-12. *The Message: The Bible in Contemporary Language*. Colorado Springs, CO: NavPress, 2002.
13. 1 John 4:8. *Revised Standard Version of the Bible*. Division of Christian Education of the National Council of the Churches of Christ in the United States of America, 1971.
14. John 3:16. *The Message: The Bible in Contemporary Language*. Colorado Springs, CO: NavPress, 2002.
15. John 3:17. *The Message: The Bible in Contemporary Language*. Colorado Springs, CO: NavPress, 2002.
16. Ephesians 4:15. *Revised Standard Version of the Bible*. Division of Christian Education of the National Council of the Churches of Christ in the United States of America, 1971. [Paraphrase mine].
17. Mandela, Nelson. www.forbes.com/ sites/ mfonobongnsehe/ 2013/ 12/06/ 20—inspirational—quotes—from—nelson—mandela.

Chapter Ten

Refresh the Power of Culture

1. James 4:1-2, 3, 8, 12. *The Message: The Bible in Contemporary Language*. Colorado Springs, CO: NavPress, 2002.
2. 1 Peter 3:15 [Paraphrase mine].
3. Armin C. Oldsen, speaker on the national radio program *The Lutheran Hour*.
4. Callahan, North. *Carl Sandburg: His Life and Works*. University Park, PA: Pennsylvania State University Press, 1987, p. 197.
5. *The Founder*, FilmNation Entertainment, The Combine, Faliro House Productions S.A., 2016.
6. *Mayflower Compact*, 1620. www.britannica.com/topic/Mayflower-Compact.
7. Quote attributed to Mahatma Gandhi.
8. Abraham Lincoln's Proclamation Appointing a National Fast Day, March 30, 1863. http://www.abrahamlincolnonline.org/lincoln/ speeches/fast.htm.
9. Message at the entrance of Utilidor—the underground tunnel into the city at Walt Disney World, Orlando, FL.
10. Galatians 5:22-23. *Revised Standard Version of the Bible*. Division of Christian Education of the National Council of the Churches of Christ in the United States of America, 1971.

Call a Church Doctor

Are you frustrated that your church isn't growing?

Is it starting to feel less like a ministry and more like a country club?

Do you feel like all your efforts yield little fruit?

As a nonprofit Christian ministry, we offer proven strategies to help Christians, pastors, and ministry leaders become more effective at their mission: the Great Commission.

Affect Life Change

Our methods help your church grow both deep and wide. Reach the unchurched in your social network, while guiding people into a deeper relationship with Jesus.

Increase Health & Vitality

Track the improvement in your church using our 9 measurable metrics that gauge health, vitality, giving, attitudes, and spiritual growth.

Reduce Stress & Burnout

Our proven proccess takes the pressure and stress off of your leadership. With ongoing support, you will never feel overwhelmed or confused about what strategy to take.

Here's how it works

Discover

First, tell us about your church or ministry. What is working? What is not? What is God's vision for your church?

Diagnose

We will help you identify the ceilings and roadblocks that are holding you or your church back. Based on 40 years of experience, we can quickly recognize trends and give you insights into how things will unfold.

Prescribe

We guide you in crafting an action plan to break through the ceilings and roadblocks and achieve your goals. We hold our clients accountable to ensure their goals are met.

You deserve a strategy to follow that will get results for your church. Partner with a Church Doctor and break through the barriers that have held you back.

CLARIFY YOUR MINISTRY MESSAGE

Focused Message + Disciplined Strategy = Mission Momentum

Your formula for clear communication, expanded influence, and increased joy in ministry

Cast a Clear & Compelling Vision

Clarify your mission and message and watch your church grow in health and vitality.

Increase Engagement

Clear communication in ministry allows more people to connect with who you are and what you do.

Reduce Friction & Frustration

Find joy in ministry again and stop spinning your wheels with outdated methods.

We know how difficult it is for a church to communicate in a noisy, distracted world. That is why we focus only on serving churches and nonprofit ministries. We know you. We have your back.

(1)	(2)	(3)	(4)
Schedule a Call	Create a Customized Communication Plan	Take Action	Ongoing Coaching and Follow-Up

Visit www.churchdoctor.org/clarify

Talk to a Guide: 800.626.8515